AF579097

PRAISE FOR *DIGITAL DANGER*

"Yes, you are the target of cybercriminals. No one knows them better than Dr. Eric Cole, and *Digital Danger* is the handbook you need today to defend yourself and secure your information."

—ROBERT WALLACE, FORMER DIRECTOR, CIA OFFICE OF TECHNICAL SERVICE

"*Digital Danger* is a wake-up call wrapped in actionable wisdom. Dr. Eric Cole turns chaos into clarity and gives every reader the power to thrive, not just survive, in the age of AI."

—JOSH LINKNER, FIVE-TIME TECH ENTREPRENEUR, *NEW YORK TIMES* BESTSELLING AUTHOR, AND VENTURE CAPITALIST

"Dr. Eric Cole once again delivers a clear-eyed, urgent road map for navigating the rapidly evolving intersection of AI and cybersecurity. A must-read for any leader responsible for protecting data, people, and digital trust in the years ahead."

—TIM STOREY, ACCLAIMED AUTHOR, SPEAKER, ADVISOR, AND LIFE COACH

"AI isn't just transforming the world—it's also opening dangerous new doors. Dr. Eric Cole's latest work cuts through the hype and lays out what's real, what's risky, and how we can reclaim control."

— PAUL ANDRE, MANAGING PARTNER, SILICON VALLEY OFFICE, AND HEAD OF INTELLECTUAL PROPERTY, US, AT HSF KRAMER

"Cybersecurity in the age of AI will separate the prepared from the compromised. Dr. Eric Cole's new book is your playbook for staying on the right side of that line."

—GARRETT WHITE, FOUNDER, WAKE UP WARRIOR

DR. ERIC COLE

DIGITAL DANGER

AI, Cybersecurity, *and the* Fight for Our Future

www.amplifypublishinggroup.com

Digital Danger: AI, Cybersecurity, and the Fight for Our Future

The advice and strategies found within may not be suitable for every situation. This work is sold with the understanding that neither the author nor the publisher is held responsible for the results accrued from the advice in this book. The publisher and the author assume no responsibility for errors, inaccuracies, omissions, or any other inconsistencies herein. All such instances are unintentional and the author's own.

All statements of fact, opinion, or analysis expressed are those of the author and do not reflect the official positions or views of the US Government. Nothing in the contents should be construed as asserting or implying US Government authentication of information or endorsement of the author's views.

For more information, please contact:
Amplify Publishing, an imprint of Amplify Publishing Group
620 Herndon Parkway, Suite 220
Herndon, VA 20170
info@amplifypublishing.com

Library of Congress Control Number: 2025926541

CPSIA Code: PRV0326A

ISBN-13: 979-8-89138-952-6

Printed in the United States

Dedicated to my amazing family, who always provides love and support.

CONTENTS

INTRODUCTION

"NOT MY PROBLEM"— WHY MOST PEOPLE DON'T SEE THE THREAT

If you are like most people, you probably spend your days scrolling the internet, making purchases on your phone, or posting to social media, all while thinking you are perfectly safe from any kind of cyberattack. That's because you are probably someone without a great amount of wealth or sensitive information, and you think no one is interested in it.

But I'm here to tell you this: You are a target, and cybersecurity is your responsibility.

Mary and Bob didn't think they had to worry, either. They were able to finally buy the dream house they'd had on their vision board for twenty years. Due to an inheritance of $1.5 million, they had the money and so made an offer, and the offer was accepted. Their excitement, joy, and thankfulness could not be described in words. It was all coming together. It seemed like nothing could go wrong and all was right with the universe.

Three days before closing, they received an email from the closing company with the wiring instructions for the money. This email was not unexpected, as they'd been told something like this was going to happen. They sent a few emails in response to verify and make sure the request was correct and accurate. Mary and Bob were well-educated people who understood the sensitivity of major transactions, so they checked and verified the transfer information. Unfortunately, through no fault of their own, they were not trained on the dangers of cyberspace.

They transferred the $1.5 million and continued to pack up their house, getting ready for moving day. They even drove past their new house, thinking about some of the upgrades they were going to make.

The day of closing arrived, and they showed up to the closing, thinking that in two hours they would have the keys and that they would be sleeping in their new house that evening.

Instead, their entire universe was about to collapse on top of them. At closing, the agent asked, "Do you have the check? We assumed you decided to bring a check, since you did not transfer the amount." Mary and Bob looked at each other, looked at the agent, and explained that they'd transferred the money already. They even had an email as proof of transfer.

It took the agent only one look at their email for him to realize that the email had not come from him and that the money had gone to the wrong bank account. As reality set in and the horror of the situation became real, Mary and Bob realized they had been scammed. Because it was now more than forty-eight hours after the transfer and they'd knowingly transferred the money, the bank was not at fault, and they were unable to recover any of their funds. That began a long, painstaking legal process to try to get their money back. That journey would take over two years and cause more heartbreak and pain than any human should have to endure. And instead of living in their dream home for those two years, they went through hell.

Even as I write about Mary and Bob's story, my hands are

shaking, and I am getting emotional, because this does not have to happen. It should not happen. But people have not been sufficiently informed about technology, and specifically about how to make it your friend rather than your enemy. The reason I wrote this book is to prevent more cases like Mary and Bob's—to secure lives.

Stories like Mary and Bob's are not uncommon. Someone tells me a story of this type of scam at least once a week. I do not hear about every case, of course, so if I hear of them weekly, it is likely happening daily or even hourly.

The solution to the kind of scam Mary and Bob fell victim to is fairly simple. Do not trust email, and do not trust any electronic form of communication. Email can be easily spoofed, and no authentication typically occurs for emails or text messages. For large amounts of money, picking up the phone to verify information, or even going in person to verify that the email you received is legitimate, will save you from heartbreak. Bring a check or verify the information in person, with a printed letter that is signed and notarized, so you can prove that authenticity of the information.

Yet this advice, while it could have saved Mary and Bob, is only one part of a broader approach to a cybersecurity tool kit that you need to implement in your life. The rest of this book will give you the tools you need to fully protect yourself in an age of accelerating cybersecurity threats and the evolving dangers artificial intelligence (AI) adds to the equation.

EVERYONE'S A TARGET—EVEN ME

I began my career as a professional hacker for the US Central Intelligence Agency (CIA), understanding and learning about how attackers break into systems and focusing on the means and methods for exploitation. I have worked in cybersecurity for decades. But even I'm susceptible to cybersecurity attacks.

I got a text from the Virginia Department of Motor Vehicles stating that they'd been notified by E-ZPass that I had unpaid tolls and that they'd tried to unsuccessfully notify me via mail. My license would be revoked soon if I didn't pay. I had recently bought a new car and had yet to transfer over my account, but I figured they would just charge my card on file. Plus, I do things electronically, so I do not check my paper mail, which meant that I could have missed a bill. The text seemed plausible. It also came later in the day, when I was tired and rushing between meetings.

While I do not like to admit it, in a moment of emotional weakness, I clicked on the link in the text. However, when I clicked on the link, the site asked for my birthday and last four digits of my Social Security number—not my license plate. At that point all the red flags went off in my mind. I quickly closed the page. I should not have clicked, but I slowed down my actions and thankfully was not a victim.

If you ever receive a suspicious text message like I did, just pause and think things through. The initial text might have tricked you the way it tricked me, but before you enter any personal data or financial data, take a few deep breaths, pause for 60 to 120 seconds, and just ask yourself, "Does this make sense?" The reality is that most victims I work with tell me that after they hit submit and after they actually provide personal or financial data, they quickly realize they are being scammed. But by the time they do, it is too late. Adding in a small delay will let your brain do what it is supposed to do—process the information and detect fraud.

THE "NO" PERSON

Over the course of my career, I've seen how cybersecurity has evolved. In the 1990s, no one understood it. If you went to an event or a party in 1998 and said you work in cybersecurity and that you are a professional hacker, you were the weird person, the person people were afraid of and thought could do harm.

Today, on the other hand, when I say I work in cybersecurity, I am the cool kid on the block, and everyone wants to talk with me. That's because everyone is beginning to understand the increasing risk of cyberattacks. However, I am still viewed as the "no" person: the person who is going to tell you that you cannot do something. While that might have been true when I started out, it is not true today.

Today, my role as your trusted advisor in cybersecurity is never to tell you yes or no but to make sure you are an educated consumer. Whether I am working with teachers, parents, or corporate executives, my job is to give you choices and make sure you are making an educated decision. Because whether you do something or not is not my concern. My concern is that you fully understand the risks you are taking and that you accept those risks should you choose to move forward with a decision. (Note: I will be using the terms *security* and *cybersecurity* interchangeably throughout the book, based on what aspect—either digital security or your overall security—I want to emphasize.)

Becoming educated starts by asking two questions: 1) "What is the true value or benefit from making this decision?" and 2) "What is the risk or exposure?" After asking those two questions, your analysis becomes simple: "Is the value or benefit worth the risk?" If it is, do it. If not, don't do it. It really is that simple. What's interesting about this decision-making frame is that it is the same advice Warren Buffett provides in investing. Warren always recommends reducing the risk and maximizing the return. When making an investment, he always asks, "Is the downside or risks worth the benefit?" This is the reason he never invested in Bitcoin or cyber currency—the risk is too great.

To understand how this logic plays out, consider how our perceptions of Alexa have changed. When Alexa devices first came out, everyone bought them. It was cool to have a device in your house that is listening to you (yes, it is listening to you 24/7) and responding to your commands. "Alexa, what is the weather?" or "Alexa, play this music."

However, everything changed when people realized Alexa was recording everything they were saying. Imagine having a bug in your house, placed by a nefarious actor, that is listening to and recording all your conversations. This realization freaked people out, and many people turned off their Alexa or limited its locations in their home.

YOU DON'T NEED TO FEEL HELPLESS

I am tired of innocent people, good people, being victimized and feeling helpless. Cybersecurity threats are a real problem, but they also have a real solution. This book will provide it. It will give you the tools to protect your life. But it all starts with awareness. If you are not aware and believe a problem exists, you cannot protect against it.

The internet was created for good, as a tool for collaboration. A tool for worldwide communication. I believe it was meant to bring humans together, to help people all around the world understand each other, resolve differences, and heal the world from the hurt and anger. However, over the years it has become a tool for evil, for causing harm, and for causing damage to innocent people—people who deserve love and respect instead of being targeted and victimized.

The reality is that using the internet involves no authentication and validation processes. Anyone can send messages to anyone. With AI, it is easy for the attacker to produce communication that is malicious but looks legitimate and is very hard for people to detect. Therefore, the number of people falling victim to attack is increasing at an exponential rate. US consumers reported losing $12.5 billion to fraud in 2024—a 25 percent increase from 2023.* The median (typical) loss per consumer fraud report in 2024 was $497.† The global average cost of a data breach in 2025 was $4.44 million.‡ The "human element" was involved in approximately 60 percent of breaches, with credential abuse and social actions like phishing among the major factors; ransomware appeared in 44 percent of breaches.§

Your probability of either one day being a victim of a cyberattack or already having been a victim of a cyberattack is as close to 100 percent as you can get. Many people are compromised, their data stolen, but since they see no visible signs or any direct impact, they do not even realize it. Just a few months prior to writing this book, over sixteen billion passwords were compromised. What made this breach so devastating is that it was not

---

* "New FTC Data Show a Big Jump in Reported Losses to Fraud to $12.5 Billion in 2024," Federal Trade Commission, March 10, 2025, https://www.ftc.gov/news-events/news/press-releases/2025/03/new-ftc-data-show-big-jump-reported-losses-fraud-125-billion-2024.

† *Consumer Sentinel Network Data Book 2024*, Federal Trade Commission, 2025, 19, https://www.ftc.gov/system/files/ftc_gov/pdf/csn-annual-data-book-2024.pdf.

‡ *Cost of a Data Breach Report 2025*, IBM Security, August 2025, https://www.ibm.com/reports/data-breach.

§ *2025 Data Breach Investigations Report—Infographic (Key Findings)*, Verizon, June 2025, https://www.verizon.com/business/resources/infographics/2025-dbir-infographic.pdf.

caused because a large company's database of users was compromised. It was done by stealing passwords from individual devices.

Unfortunately, this breach happened twenty-four hours before the US attack on Iran, so most people never heard about it—the story got buried, and innocent people are now walking around with compromised devices, compromised accounts, and compromised passwords. Also, we get a device like a smartphone and use the same version for years, which means that if it is compromised, it will stay compromised for a long time. Therefore, it is important to periodically reimagine your device with a clean, secure version of the operating system.

WHY YOU ARE A TARGET

The attacker—or what I call "the enemy"—is looking for opportunities to target you, to hurt you, and to ruin your life. The attacker is not fair; they are ruthless and will exploit you when you least expect it. And they know a lot more about your life than you realize. Through the internet, so much information is publicly available, but many people do not realize it or how exposed they are. Knowing where to look, you can find out information about anyone, anytime, anyplace.

The number one comment I hear from people is "I am too small to be targeted by an attacker. Attackers only go after the rich and famous, who have millions or billions of dollars. They are not going to target me—I only have $10,000 or $50,000 in my bank account." The reality is that *you* are who they want to target because your guard is down and you are more vulnerable and easier to steal from.

If I am an attacker, I want to go after the targets that allow for the biggest payoff for the least amount of effort. Twenty years ago, they targeted big companies, because they had large databases of information and relatively weak security. So, if I went after a big bank or a big tech company, I could get in relatively easily since they were missing patches or had known vulnerabilities—I could download fifty million records and be done. However, today most companies have implemented more robust security measures. Now, as an attacker I could target a big company with a hundred million records (and yes, it does happen), but the reality is that such companies are spending $20 million on security and have fifty people working in cybersecurity to monitor, defend against, and detect attacks. This type of attack could take six to nine months, and attackers face a high chance of getting caught and a low probability of being successful.

Or I could target two million consumers, people who do not think they are a target, people who have no dedicated security team, and steal ten dollars from each, or even a hundred dollars. If this were done over several months, most people would not even notice it or detect it.

Let's be honest, if you went to a restaurant and the bill was around seventy dollars and you left a fifteen-dollar tip, you do not actually record the exact amount. At the end of the month, if you see a charge for the restaurant for ninety or ninety-five dollars, you would probably not give it a second thought. This is how the current cybercriminal works and operates.

Accessing your personal information is also a big business for the enemy. Your information is being bought and sold on the dark web. The dark web is simply a version of the internet that is isolated from the public internet, requires special browsers to access, and is known for anonymity. Today it has become the trading ground for anything stolen or illegal.

If you want to buy or sell passwords or corporate data, this is the place attackers go to monetize their attack. People often ask, "What value does someone get from stealing passwords or stealing my data?" The reality is that people are willing to pay for it. Here is a brief breakdown of the price for passwords on the dark web:

- *Streaming-service accounts*: Typically priced between ninety cents and two dollars for services like Netflix, Disney+, and Hulu.
- *Hacked social media accounts*: Prices vary, with some being sold for as low as a dollar and others fetching up to sixty dollars. Accounts with a strong reputation, like an eBay account, can go for as much as $1,000.
- *Online banking logins*: Prices average around thirty-five dollars, often including login details, name and address of the account holder, and instructions on how to access the account undetected. Accounts with higher balances or in banks with fewer security measures may be more expensive.
- *Email accounts*: A hacked Gmail account can be bought for approximately eighty dollars.
- *Cash App login credentials*: These are significantly more expensive, carrying an average price of $860.
- *General online credentials*: Prices typically range from one dollar to five dollars per account.

Your password, your data, and your life are worth a lot of money. That is the reason that you are a target. This problem will only get worse before it gets better.

Adding to this problem is that using, taking, and correlating this data is technically not illegal. The cyber laws are not consistent around the world and often are not sufficient to keep up with crime. And to make matters worse, the United States is one of the few countries in the world that does not have unified federal laws on cybersecurity and data privacy, which makes US citizens a prime target.

AI AND CYBERSECURITY

Today I cringe when I hear tech executives say that AI is going to replace 40 percent of the workforce or that AI is going to make humans irrelevant or extinct. I personally take offense to these statements—not only because they devalue human labor but also because saying that AI will replace humans is the same as saying that humans are a lower form of intelligence. This forgets that humans have emotions, humans have feelings, humans have organs and real brains—things that computers will never ever have. Have you ever been down and have gotten a real, genuine hug? There is no way AI or any computer can ever do that. So, unless we are saying that humans are dumb and can be manipulated by computers, to me these statements are naive and do not understand just how powerful and amazing humans really are.

We as humans must not accept AI to do human-related tasks. Tasks that require someone to care, someone to have emotions, and someone to understand someone's struggle should never be replaced by a computer. Some companies, to save a buck, might try to replace genuine human labor with AI, but we cannot let them. If I have a problem and want to talk with a human who can emotionally connect with me, and a company does not allow me to do this, I will not do business with them. If we as humans unite and don't let big tech question our humanity, AI can be a resource to help us. It can be a friend, not an enemy.

And that is the point of this book. I am a huge tech person—I love AI and use AI on a daily basis. But it is a tool to help me be more effective, not a replacement for who I am and what I can do. Not a single page in this book was generated by AI—that would be insulting to you as a reader and to me, implying that my knowledge acquired over thirty-plus years can be replaced by an AI tool searching generic information on the internet.

Despite the limitations of AI, it is rapidly becoming the most important force multiplier in cybersecurity because the scale, speed, and sophistication of today's threats far exceed what humans can process alone. Every second, billions of digital signals are generated—emails sent, logins attempted, transactions processed, and packets transmitted across networks. Hidden in that ocean of data are subtle anomalies that point to phishing attacks, insider threats, malware infections, or advanced persistent intrusions. Traditional tools, designed around fixed rules and signatures, simply cannot keep up. Attackers are constantly evolving, using automation and AI themselves to probe for weaknesses and launch attacks that adapt in real time. Without AI, defenders are left trying to fight modern cyberwars with outdated weapons. With AI, cybersecurity teams can automatically sift through massive datasets, detect patterns invisible to the human eye, and identify threats at machine speed before damage is done.

But AI's role goes beyond defense—it also represents the only path forward for truly proactive cybersecurity. Instead of reacting to incidents after they occur, AI enables predictive models that forecast where the next attack will strike and recommend defenses before vulnerabilities are exploited. It can simulate potential attack paths, stress test systems automatically, and even orchestrate real-time responses without waiting for human intervention. In many ways, AI is the nervous system of modern cyber defense: constantly sensing, analyzing, and reacting to keep digital environments safe. The stakes are high—without AI, organizations risk being permanently outpaced by adversaries. With AI, they gain the ability not just to survive but to thrive in an increasingly hostile digital landscape. In short, AI is not just an enhancement to cybersecurity; it is becoming the foundation that future digital trust and resilience will be built upon.

SAFE DRIVERS, NOT SAFE CARS

You can have the safest car on the planet, but if you do not have a safe driver, it does not matter. If a driver is not paying attention, they can still get into an accident, still cause harm to themselves and harm to others, no matter how many safety features are in the car. This is why, if you get pulled over for reckless driving, the number one recommendation of the court will be for you to take a safe driving course—not to get a safer car. Safe drivers keep the roads safe, not safe cars.

The internet and the digital world are no different. You can have a relatively safe computer, but if you click on links or open attachments, you can still be infected and still get compromised. I am often challenged when I give keynotes on whether we can actually achieve 100 percent security. I say, "Sure, but here's how. I can take your computer, wipe all the drives, smash it into pieces, and give it an acid bath so that the pieces are completely disintegrated. That device is now 100 percent secure. However, it is completely and totally useless. For the technology to have value, it must have functionality, which means that we will have vulnerabilities that can be exploited."

A great example is a smartphone: iPhone or Android—both are similar. If I take an iPhone out of the box, it is fairly secure and locked down and difficult to break into it. Assuming you follow the instructions and update the iOS, you have an updated system with minimal functionality and a high degree of security. Now, if you kept it that way, you would be fairly secure, but it would have minimal value to you, because what does everyone do once they have an iPhone? Install apps, more apps, and more apps, many of which you probably have not used in six months and do not really need.

While simple devices like smartphones are fairly secure out of the box, that logic does not apply to operating systems or websites or apps. The good news is that cybersecurity is a top priority for companies. Almost every operating system and cloud provider and website has robust security measures built in, but unfortunately they are turned off. The reason is that developers do not think consumers want to deal with the perceived inconvenience created by the limited functionality of the security. One of my missions is to convince big tech and get federal laws passed that say security must be turned on by default, and if someone wants to be attacked and vulnerable, they can turn it off. But my guess is that when I achieve my mission and make security a default, most people won't opt out.

We see this with automobiles: Seat belts, airbags, and antilock brakes are turned on and standard in many cars. People accept them, use them, and appreciate them. They do not try to turn off antilock brakes or remove airbags. With the digital world, we need to get to this level of security to make sure we are creating safe drivers on the information superhighway and technology that is secure out of the box.

AN ACTION PLAN

The reality is that we spend most of our lives online in a digital world. This might shock some people, but globally the average person spends six hours and forty minutes online a day, and in the United States, that number is just over seven hours.

We teach our kids to look both ways before crossing a street and to not get into a car with strangers. We also train our kids to not eat food off the ground or from someone they do not know. Yet we have given ourselves and our kids technology, providing little to no training, and use apps that violate these rules.

This book is the equivalent of what we teach our kids as they are learning about the world. But we have already been living our lives online—some of us for over a decade—without these rules and safety tips. We do not know how to look both ways while crossing the street or to not eat food off the sidewalk. We do not have the basics, much less the advanced tips to keep us safe.

I will offer you both: how to get started with cybersecurity as well as how to become an expert. The rest of the book will walk you through not only what you need to know about the current state of cybersecurity in a world driven by AI but also what specific steps you can take for each of your connected devices. Once you finish this book and implement my recommendations, you'll be safer—both online and off.

CHAPTER 1

UNDERSTANDING THE PROBLEM—HOW AI AMPLIFIES THREATS AND GOVERNMENT LETS US DOWN

When people picture cybercrime, they often imagine a hoodie in a dark room, green code streaming down a screen, and government command centers humming in the background. In my career, the real danger almost never looks like that. It looks like ordinary people in ordinary rooms—cafeterias, fellowship halls, conference rooms—who never got the instruction manual for the world they're living in.

One Tuesday night, a local parent-teacher association asked me to share "a few quick tips" about keeping kids safe online. It was winter. Coats were piled on the backs of folding chairs. Someone had set out a tray of store-bought cookies and a box of coffee. Parents filtered in after work, juggling dinner, homework, and rides to practice. I expected a polite listen. I got something else: urgency.

We started simply—what children post, who sees it, and how criminals build trust by pretending to be peers. Within minutes, hands shot up.

A father told me his middle schooler had clicked a link in a group chat about a "limited-time gaming upgrade." It looked like an offer from the game developer, complete with the right logo and color palette. His son typed in the family credit card and the login he uses for "everything." They didn't just lose money; attackers took that password and tried it on their email, their streaming accounts, and—yes—their bank. The father's voice shook because he realized how close they'd come to losing the family's savings.

A mother admitted she'd seen "VPN" on her daughter's phone and thought it was a social app. Her daughter explained—confidently—that it "just helps with school Wi-Fi." But VPN actually stands for "virtual private network." Her daughter didn't mention how VPNs help users bypass filters and mask a location or how it can be a tool for hiding risky behavior—bypassing parental controls. Mom wasn't angry; she was stunned that the language her family used every day—apps, accounts, followers—had outpaced the rules of the house.

Then a teacher asked a quiet question: "Can someone turn on a webcam without the light?" You could feel the room inhale. People weren't asking for configuration guides. They were asking if the world was as dangerous as it felt.

And the answer is *yes*.

After the Q&A session, two lines formed. One was for general questions—passwords, iCloud, "Do I need antivirus?" The other was private. A mother waited in tears that she kept wiping away. Her daughter had sent someone a photo that she had never meant to share beyond a circle of "friends." The profile of this person belonged to someone who had changed their name three times in a month. The initial messages were bad enough; however, this escalated to threats: Pay, send more, or they would send the image to classmates and relatives. The mother kept saying, "We're good people. We didn't think like this." That sentence has echoed in my head ever since.

The next night, I spoke at a church on the other side of town. Different crowd, same questions. An older couple had wired

$9,800 to "their grandson" who was "in legal trouble" in Mexico. The call sounded exactly like him—same tone, same cadence, the little phrase he says when he's nervous. They didn't know voice cloning was possible. They hung their heads as if they had failed a moral test, when in truth they had been targeted by professionals who weaponize human compassion.

A week later, I sat with a corporate board. These were seasoned executives, people who handle risk daily. We reviewed an incident where an employee received a request to change a vendor's payment details. The "vendor" wrote in perfect English, referenced a real project, and sent a PDF with the exact template the company uses. The accounts payable team made the update. Hundreds of thousands of dollars were routed to an account overseas. When the board asked, "Who in government do we call to get this money back?" the room went quiet. They realized there isn't a 911 for the internet.

Those three rooms—PTA, church, and boardroom—are where this book begins. Not with hackers in basements but with families and organizations standing on digital quicksand, assuming someone else poured a foundation of concrete. We've been living as if the internet is a friendly utility. It isn't. It's a frontier where the same tools that make life convenient can be aimed back at us with precision, speed, and scale—especially now that artificial intelligence is part of the attacker's kit.

Two truths frame everything that follows. First, attacks are rising because our rules, roles, and laws have not kept pace—and our government systems remain fragmented. Second, AI amplifies old tricks and invents new ones, making scams more convincing, faster, and harder to detect. If that sounds bleak, stay with me. Understanding the problem is the first act of defense. You can't fix what you won't name.

THE TWO ENGINES DRIVING TODAY'S SURGE IN ATTACKS

1. *Government fragmentation*: Cyber responsibility is scattered across agencies with overlapping mandates and different priorities. We've built a maze when we needed a highway. Attackers move in minutes; we coordinate in months. That gap is a gift to criminals and hostile states.
2. *AI amplification*: Everything criminals already did—phishing, social engineering, credential stuffing, payment fraud—scales with AI. Messages read like a native speaker wrote them. Voice and video can be cloned. Attacks iterate automatically. The same technology that lets your phone recognize your face can be used to impersonate your child. AI has not created any new attacks or threats; it has just allowed the existing attacks to be done with more precision and more accuracy. In some cases, this AI amplification makes it impossible for the average person to catch or stop, giving the adversary the ultimate upper hand.

The combination of these two trends is combustible: slow defenders and fast attackers, confusion at the top and automation at the bottom, public complacency and private vulnerability.

PLAIN-ENGLISH GLOSSARY: THE WORDS THAT MATTER

Before we dive deeper, let's level the language. Jargon creates distance. Clarity creates power. Here are distinctions I want you to carry through the rest of the book—explained the way I explain them to PTAs, churches, and boards:

- *Cyber*: Anything touching computers, networks, or the internet. If it plugs in and talks to something else, it's in cyber territory.
- *Digital*: Electronic or computerized in general. A digital photo on your camera that never leaves the device is digital; it becomes a cyber issue when you sync or share it.
- *Cloud*: Someone else's computer. Your files live on servers you don't see, owned by companies you may not know, in locations that might be across the country—or across the world.
- *Data*: The "stuff" of your life and business—photos, invoices, medical records, school transcripts, tax returns. Data is the prize attackers want.
- *Cybersecurity*: a) The practice of protecting systems, networks, and data from attack. Think locks, alarms, and cameras—except for your digital property; b) understanding, managing, and mitigating the risk of critical assets being disclosed, altered, or denied access.
- *Privacy*: Control over who sees your data and how it's used. Security keeps the door locked; privacy decides who you invite in.

- *Identity theft*: When someone uses your personal details (SSN, date of birth, address) to pose as you—opening accounts, taking out loans, or committing crimes.
- *Phishing*: Impersonation over email to get you to click, pay, or reveal secrets. *Smishing* is the text message version; *vishing* uses voice calls.
- *Malware*: Malicious software. Ransomware locks your files and demands payment; spyware watches; keyloggers record what you type.
- *Ransomware*: A type of malware attack that locks you out of a system or program (or threatens to release incriminating information on you) unless you pay a certain amount of money.
- *Multi-factor authentication* (*MFA*): A second proof that it's really you (a code, an app prompt, a key). It turns a stolen password into a speed bump instead of a master key. Note that this is sometimes called two-factor authentication (2FA), which is a subset of MFA that uses just two factors.
- *Encryption*: Scrambling data so only the right people can read it. Like putting your words into a locked safe and handing out only the correct keys.
- *Virtual private network* (*VPN*): A secure tunnel for your internet connection. It can protect privacy on public Wi-Fi, but it won't fix bad passwords or stop you from clicking a bad link. And as we saw in the above examples, anything that can be used for good can be used for evil.

- *Zero-day*: A software flaw the maker doesn't yet know about. Attackers love zero-days because nobody has a patch for them—yet.
- *Botnet*: A herd of hacked devices—laptops, webcams, even doorbells—controlled by an attacker to send spam, break websites, or run scams at scale.
- *Deepfake/voice clone*: AI-made video or audio that looks and sounds real but isn't. Today, a thirty-second clip of your voice can be enough to copy it convincingly.
- *Social engineering*: Hacking the human, not the computer. It exploits trust, authority, urgency, and empathy to get you to do what the attacker wants. It is by far the most common and effective attack on the market today.
- *Endpoint*: Any device that touches your network—phones, laptops, tablets, servers. If it's an endpoint, it's a doorway. Doors need locks.

You don't have to memorize these. Keep them handy. When the terms make sense, what you encounter makes sense—and so do your choices.

HOW GAPS IN LAW AND GOVERNMENT CREATE OPENINGS FOR ATTACKERS

One reason the PTA, the church congregation, and the corporate board I met all felt powerless is that they assumed there was a reliable, well-oiled safety net. Call the right number, file the right form, and the cavalry shows up. In the physical world, we've built that. In the digital world, we haven't. The internet erased borders; our laws did not. As of the writing of this book, the United States is one of the few countries in the world that do not have unified federal laws on cybersecurity and data privacy. And if federal laws do not even exist, there cannot be any attempt at federal or international enforcement and prosecution.

Borders on Paper, Borderless in Practice

If someone kicks in your front door, that person will be dealt with through criminal statutes, local officers, and a sentencing framework, all of which have been in place for generations. If someone in another country empties your bank account with a keyboard, which law applies? Whose police? Which judge? What if the attacker is in a place that won't cooperate—or where the country looks the other way when its "patriotic hackers" aim at foreign targets?

Cybercrime found the seams to break through long before governments stitched them. Consider three moments that made the world blink:

1. *A nation under DDoS*: Starting in 2024 and continuing today, a wave of attacks crashed the public websites of a small European country's banks, media outlets, and government agencies. The world realized that a keyboard could make a nation flinch. Today, as I am editing this chapter, cybercriminals took down the computers at major airports in Europe, delaying flights and impacting air traffic control systems. Was it crime? War? Protest? The answer mattered—because different answers trigger different authorities, treaties, and responses. The legal vocabulary was—and still is—behind the facts on the ground.

2. *Ransomware crosses oceans in hours*: A fast-moving piece of malicious code locked files across continents, from hospitals to factories. The hackers would only unlock the files if the victim paid a ransom. Depending on the size of the company, ransom payments ranged from $50,000 to $5 million. Victims faced a grim choice: pay criminals or shut down essential services. Courts could argue about liability later; patients and payroll couldn't wait. When a weapon spreads faster than any legal process can move, criminals have leverage.
3. *Personnel records stolen at scale*: Sensitive background records—forms, fingerprints, histories—were copied and exfiltrated from a US system. Millions of identities, including national security personnel, were exposed. Which border did the theft cross? All of them. Who owns the remedy? Anyone's guess. The original attack was against Equifax and occurred in 2017, with 147 million personal records stolen. While this attack happened many years ago, the impact is still felt today. Imagine living your life with your Social Security and birth date publicly known to attackers. This is not information that can be easily changed.

What ties these moments together is not novelty but jurisdiction. Our enforcement tools are bound by geography. The internet is not.

The "Too Many Cooks" Problem

Inside the United States, responsibility for cyber is spread across multiple agencies that each own a slice of the problem:

- FBI investigates cybercrime and nation-state intrusions.
- CISA (Homeland Security) focuses on protecting critical infrastructure and issuing alerts.
- NSA handles intelligence and defense of certain federal systems.
- Secret Service investigates financial cybercrime.
- FTC, SEC, HHS, Department of Education, state AGs, and others regulate specific sectors and enforce privacy/security rules.

No one is focused on educating the public and keeping citizens aware, safe from attacks.

I began my career as a professional hacker for the CIA and had the opportunity to work with the Nuclear Regulatory Commission (NRC) on securing nuclear reactors. I also worked at Lockheed Martin as a chief scientist and senior fellow. From there I was chief technology officer at McAfee and then built and ran the cyber defense curriculum for the SANS Institute. You can find out more about me at www.drericcole.com. Throughout all my work, I have seen that no one is responsible for informing the public, educating the public, and raising awareness. This is why I am America's self-appointed cyber czar, because I am beyond tired and frustrated that no one cares about you or your loved ones when they are victims of cybercrime.

I've sat in rooms where company leaders ask government

officials, "Who do we call?" after an attack and heard three different answers from well-meaning officials—each correct in a narrow sense but insufficient alone. Agencies do collaborate; professionals in those seats work hard. But the structure itself creates friction when what we need is flow. Attackers exploit that delay.

Politics over Protection

Cybersecurity thrives on consistency: baselines, exercises, rehearsals, and muscle memory. Our politics thrive on cycles: budget fights, leadership changes, and shifting priorities. Every time a program is launched, paused, rebranded, or defunded, attackers get a head start. They don't hold press conferences. They don't wait for rule making. They don't need a quorum.

I've watched capable teams lose months to process while adversaries refined tools daily. I've seen leaders treat cyber as a PR issue until an outage hits the front page. I've watched critical initiatives get delayed through partisan arguments that had little to do with technical merit and everything to do with timing. When the budget line item wins over the risk reality, the adversary wins twice: fewer defenses and more complacency.

The Public-Private Seesaw

Most of what attackers hit is owned by businesses, schools, hospitals, and local governments. Most of what defenders know about exploiting and breaking into systems first lives in government sensors and intelligence. Getting the right signal to the right owner at the right time is a dance we're still learning. When it works, early warnings turn into patched systems and blocked attempts. When it doesn't, the same exploit lands in victim after victim while alerts trickle out in language too vague to act on. Most attacks today occur because of unpatched systems or users being tricked to click on links. Unfortunately, most of the attack vectors are not sophisticated, but they take advantage of weaknesses we know about but are not being fixed.

Public-private sector cooperation in cybersecurity today is marked by progress but also by fragmentation and friction. On the positive side, government agencies such as CISA, NSA, and the FBI are more active than ever in issuing alerts, threat advisories, and joint security bulletins. Large corporations, industry groups, and information-sharing platforms like Information Sharing and Analysis Centers (ISACs) and Information Sharing and Analysis Organizations (ISAOs) provide forums for exchanging technical indicators and best practices. High-profile incidents—such as ransomware attacks on hospitals, energy pipelines, or supply chains—have driven home the message that no single entity can defend alone, prompting closer coordination. Still, the reality on the ground is uneven. For most small to midsize businesses, schools, and local governments, the flow of government intelligence is still too slow, too generic, and too wrapped in classification to be actionable. At the same time, private companies hesitate to share back their own breach details, fearing reputational damage, litigation, or regulatory backlash. The result is a half-built bridge: Signals move, but not fast or clearly enough; cooperation happens, but often only after the fact. Too many organizations remain isolated, hoping they will not be next, while attackers exploit the same weaknesses across victim after victim.

Information sharing has improved in recent years, but the incentive problem remains: A company that discloses an incident can face lawsuits and headlines; a company that stays quiet can hope no one notices. We need to make it easier to share information about attacks quickly. The attacker's advantage is not just code; it's our reluctance to admit when we've been hit.

And the government overclassifies attacks, breaches, and exploits, so it is not given to the right people in the private sector to empower them to act on the information.

Fixing this dynamic requires shifting from ad hoc, compliance-driven interaction to a culture of trust, transparency, and shared responsibility. First, the government must declassify and streamline its threat intelligence pipeline so that private-sector defenders receive clear, timely, and actionable insights—not redacted fragments or vague warnings. Second, the private sector must be incentivized to report breaches and share attack data without fear of lawsuits or financial ruin; liability protections, safe-harbor rules, and clear reporting standards can create that safety net. Third, cooperation needs to extend beyond headline-grabbing incidents to continuous, routine engagement—joint exercises, cross-sector cyber drills, and shared investments in resilience. Finally, leadership at the highest levels must treat cybersecurity as a national mission, not a siloed IT problem. A genuine public-private partnership means standing on the same side of the table, fighting a common enemy with unified resources. Until that cultural and structural shift happens, attackers will continue to exploit the gaps. But if we get it right, we can turn today's fragile seesaw into a stable alliance, where intelligence moves as quickly as exploits and resilience becomes a shared asset rather than a competitive burden.

What This Means for You

All this—the jurisdiction gaps, the agency overlap, the politics, the missing baselines, the seesaw—lands on your kitchen table.

It's why the PTA room felt exposed, why the church congregants felt ashamed, and why the board looked stunned. We built a digital world where anyone, anywhere, can knock on your door, and we assumed the lock came preinstalled. But it did not.

That doesn't mean you're powerless. It means the first line of defense is closer than most people think: your choices, your settings, your habits, your culture at home and at work. It means the institutions you rely on need a push—from you—to adopt the practices that will keep your data safe when, not if, someone comes knocking. And it means we should stop waiting for a single agency, a single law, or a single technology to "solve cyber" for us. The cavalry is not coming. *We* are the cavalry.

WHY AI CHANGES THE STAKES (AND WHY WE CAN'T IGNORE IT)

If all we were facing were outdated laws and slow coordination, vigilance and commonsense controls would still carry the day. But AI changes the pace and polish of the threat. It removes the old tells—bad grammar, awkward phrasing, inconsistent voice—and replaces them with messages that sound exactly like the person you trust. It takes the one-to-one con and turns it into a one-to-many operation. It makes the timeline shorter, the evidence thinner, the doubt sharper. AI is not just another tool attackers use—it's a force multiplier that magnifies every weakness we leave unaddressed. In other words, the gap between what we think is protecting us and what actually is keeping us safe has never mattered more.

What AI Really Means in Cybersecurity

When people hear the term artificial intelligence, most picture science fiction: robots walking among us, self-aware computers, or perhaps Hollywood's favorite scenario—machines turning against their makers. That imagery makes AI feel distant, futuristic, and even optional to think about. But AI is not a future issue—it's here, and it's already transforming both everyday convenience and everyday danger.

At its core, AI is not magic. I was actively building AI models and doing AI programming in 1991 to track terrorists, and what we have today is merely an updated version of that "old school" AI. It's a way of teaching machines to recognize patterns, make predictions, and generate outputs based on vast amounts of data. It can "see" faces in photos, "hear" words in recordings, and "write" text that feels human. It can analyze millions of inputs in seconds, far faster than any person. Those qualities make it incredibly useful—and incredibly dangerous.

On the positive side, AI powers the facial recognition that unlocks your phone, filters spam from your inbox, and suggests the fastest route to work. Doctors use AI to detect early signs of cancer, farmers use it to predict crop yields, and meteorologists use it to model storms. But the very features that make AI helpful—speed, accuracy, adaptability—also make it a weapon when criminals get their hands on it.

That's the double-edged sword of AI in cybersecurity: The same tools that defend us can be turned against us.

How AI Supercharges Phishing

Phishing—the art of tricking someone into clicking a link, downloading a file, or sharing personal information—has been around since the early days of email. For decades, it was the cyber equivalent of a street con: poorly worded messages promising riches, fake bank alerts with obvious typos, or clumsy impersonations of CEOs. Many people could spot them a mile away.

AI has changed that. With modern tools, phishing emails are no longer riddled with errors. They are grammatically correct, stylistically polished, and tailored to look identical to legitimate communications. AI can do the following:

- *Write fluent, convincing text*: Emails now sound like they were written by a native speaker—or better yet, by your actual coworker or bank.
- *Personalize at scale*: Criminals can feed in information scraped from social media, LinkedIn, or public records. Instead of "Dear Customer," the email greets you by name, references your recent vacation, or mentions your employer.
- *Generate unlimited variations*: Spam filters rely on patterns. AI breaks patterns. Instead of one generic email, attackers can send thousands of slightly different versions, making them much harder to block.

Here's an example I encountered. An executive received an email that looked exactly like her bank's fraud alert. It listed her correct account number (pulled from a breached database), referenced a real transaction she'd made the day before (gleaned from leaked merchant records), and urged her to "reverify" her login to protect her account. Everything looked correct—the branding, the writing style, even the timing. She clicked, entered her credentials, and within hours, her account was drained. This wasn't luck on the attacker's part. It was AI.

Deepfakes and Voice Cloning: Fooling Eyes and Ears

If phishing attacks exploit our reading, deepfakes exploit our sight and hearing. A deepfake is audio or video that looks and sounds real but has been artificially generated.

A few years ago, deepfakes were mainly online novelties—silly videos of celebrities "singing" songs they'd never recorded or movie characters swapped into memes. But the technology has advanced with breathtaking speed. Today, deepfakes can replicate a person's face and voice with alarming accuracy.

Voice Cloning

With as little as thirty seconds of recorded speech—often grabbed from social media or YouTube—AI can generate a convincing clone of someone's voice. Criminals use this to call relatives, employees, or parents and pretend to be someone else. People post videos on social media to share with their friends, never realizing they are providing an attacker's AI the exact training data it needs to create a duplicate or deepfake containing whatever content they want them to say.

Imagine receiving a frantic call from what sounds exactly like your daughter: "Mom, please help me—I'm in trouble. Wire money now!" Would you question it? Most wouldn't. And that's why it works. As a parent, if it was real and my child was truly in danger, I would wire the money. But it is not real.

In 2023, parents in Arizona received such a call. The voice was indistinguishable from their teenage daughter's. The caller demanded ransom money, claiming she had been kidnapped. Terrified, the parents paid thousands before confirming that their daughter was safe at school. The "voice" was generated from clips pulled off the daughter's TikTok videos. And the money was gone. Most of these attacks use cryptocurrency or other means of wire transfer that are not traceable because traditional banking mechanisms are built with checks and balances in place.

Video Deepfakes

Video is no safer. Imagine you're on a Zoom call with your boss, and she tells you to approve a wire transfer. The face looks right, the voice matches, and the background even shows her office. But it's not her—it's a video deepfake.

In 2019, criminals used a voice deepfake to trick a British energy company into wiring $240,000, believing the request came from their CEO. Since then, technology has improved. Now video fakes are realistic enough to pass in casual conversations, raising the stakes for businesses and governments alike.

The scariest part? The tools to make these fakes aren't locked in secret labs. Many are free or low cost, available to anyone with a computer and an internet connection.

Automated Attacks at Scale

Before AI, most cyberattacks were labor intensive. Hackers probed networks one by one, guessed passwords manually, or wrote malware line by line. AI automates all that.

- *Password cracking*: AI can analyze millions of combinations per second, predicting likely passwords based on common patterns—birthdays, pets' names, sports teams.
- *Scanning for vulnerabilities*: AI can scan thousands of websites simultaneously, flagging weak points faster than any human team.
- *Adaptive learning*: If an attack fails, AI quickly adjusts tactics and tries again, improving with every attempt.

Imagine defending your house from a burglar. In the past, maybe one or two burglars tested your locks. Now picture thousands of burglars swarming every window and door at once, each adapting their approach as they go. That's what AI-powered cyberattacks look like.

Why AI-Driven Scams Work: The Psychology of Deception

Technology is only half the story. Cybercrime succeeds because it exploits human psychology. Criminals understand that people trust authority, act quickly under pressure, and let their guard down when something feels personal. AI makes these manipulations sharper and more convincing.

Here are the main levers attackers use:

1. *Authority*: We instinctively trust messages that appear to come from bosses, banks, or government agencies. AI makes impersonation flawless.
2. *Urgency and fear*: When told "Your account will be locked in twelve hours" or "Your child is in danger," rational thinking shuts down. Panic drives quick action.

3. *Personalization*: Messages that reference your spouse's name, your employer, or your last purchase feel authentic. AI scrapes this data easily.
4. *Repetition*: Even skeptical people can be worn down by repeated, varied attempts. AI can generate endless tries until one slips through.
5. *Bias exploitation*: We're more likely to believe messages that confirm our beliefs or fears. AI-driven disinformation campaigns exploit this on social media, polarizing communities and eroding trust.

This isn't theoretical. It's happening every day, at scale, across inboxes, phones, and feeds.

The Spiral Effect: AI That Learns

Perhaps the most alarming feature of AI in cybercrime is its ability to learn. Unlike traditional scams, which fail and fade, AI systems analyze failures and adapt.

- If one phishing email gets blocked, AI generates a new variation.
- If a deepfake looks suspicious, AI improves it until it passes.
- If a password guess fails, AI recalibrates and tries smarter.

This creates a vicious cycle: Every failed attack makes the next one stronger. Defenders aren't just fighting criminals—they're fighting algorithms that evolve.

THE DOUBLE-EDGED SWORD OF AI

Artificial intelligence is not inherently evil. In fact, it holds enormous promise. Cybersecurity defenders use AI to identify suspicious behavior faster than humans ever could.

But here's the uncomfortable truth: Criminals innovate faster. They don't worry about ethics committees, regulatory approval, or public accountability. They adopt new technology instantly if it gives them an advantage. Governments, meanwhile, are slowed by politics, budgets, and bureaucracy. Businesses hesitate, worrying about cost or public perception. That gap—between reckless innovation on the attacker side and slow adoption on the defender side—is where AI becomes a weapon.

When AI was created, few thought it could be used by criminal elements with such speed and precision. AI security was not made a priority. Now, adding security is difficult and hard and relies on you as the consumer to be informed so that you do not fall prey to these attacks.

The average citizen, family, and community become the casualty of that imbalance.

But we do not have to be. We can take control of our own security. Doing so requires a mindset shift to think about how each aspect of our digital life—from our credit cards to our texting to our steaming sites to our social media—and how it could expose us to risks. In the next chapter, I'll walk you through the risks of remaining complacent and not taking on the responsibility of your own protection yourself.

KEY TAKEAWAYS

- ☐ Cybercrime thrives on gaps. Outdated laws and uncoordinated government agencies leave openings that attackers exploit.
- ☐ AI changes the game. It makes scams more believable, attacks more scalable, and criminals more adaptive.
- ☐ Humans are the real target. Cybercrime manipulates trust, fear, urgency, and personalization to deceive.
- ☐ The costs are personal. Identity theft, drained savings, and ruined reputations devastate individuals.
- ☐ The costs ripple outward. Businesses fail, hospitals shut down, cities stall, and nations falter.
- ☐ Trust is eroding. Families, communities, and democracies cannot function when truth itself is under attack.
- ☐ The next generation will pay. If we don't act, our children will inherit the risks we ignored.
- ☐ Awareness is defense. Knowledge doesn't solve everything, but it changes everything.

CHAPTER 2

AI AND CYBERSECURITY IN BUSINESS—THE RISKS AND COSTS OF IGNORING THE PROBLEM

In 2017, one of the largest credit reporting agencies in the United States, Equifax, announced that hackers had stolen the personal data of nearly 150 million Americans. This wasn't just a cyber headline—it was a national crisis. Social Security numbers, birth dates, addresses, and financial histories were exposed.

Here's the critical point: The people affected weren't Equifax's customers. They didn't sign up for the service. They didn't hand over their data willingly. Yet their lives were turned upside down. Why? Because Equifax failed to secure its systems, and in doing so, it exposed nearly half the US population to identity theft.

Equifax is not a consumer-facing company in the traditional sense; it doesn't sell products directly to the public. Instead, it collects and aggregates personal and financial data from banks, credit card companies, lenders, and other institutions and then packages that information into credit reports and scores. That means the 147 million people whose data was exposed in the breach never chose to do business with Equifax. They didn't sign a contract, open an account, or hand over their information voluntarily. Their personal details—names, Social Security numbers, addresses, and financial histories—were swept into Equifax's databases simply because they participated in the modern economy. The breach was therefore not just an attack on a company but an attack on people who had no direct relationship with that company, highlighting a fundamental problem in how critical data is collected, stored, and secured without true consumer consent.

That breach cost Equifax more than $1.4 billion in fines, settlements, and remediation costs. But the real price was paid by ordinary people—parents, students, retirees—who suddenly had to monitor their credit, freeze accounts, and live with the anxiety that their most private information might be floating around the dark web.

This story illustrates a truth I've seen again and again in my career: When businesses ignore cybersecurity, it's the consumer who suffers the consequences. And in today's world—where AI and digital technology drive everything from finance to health care—those consequences are only getting bigger, faster, and more personal.

ACCOUNTABILITY AND STANDARDIZATION IN CYBERSECURITY

In aviation, pilots use checklists. In medicine, surgical teams run time-outs. In construction, inspectors sign off before people move in. In cyber, too many environments still lack standards for acceptable use—like enforced password hygiene, multi-factor authentication, least privilege access, immutable backups, and rehearsed incident response. We do have frameworks that outline best practices, but what's missing is adoption that sticks and accountability that bites. This cannot be fixed by the government or big tech alone. We all have to do our part, especially those businesses that are responsible for customer data.

For years, I've watched companies treat cybersecurity as a box-checking exercise—buying new tools, writing policies, and sending out generic training modules. But here's the reality: None of that matters if the leadership culture is wrong. If cybersecurity is seen as "someone else's job," companies will keep getting breached, and consumers will keep paying the price. We can't solve this problem with technology alone. What we need is accountability and standardization at the leadership level. Until that happens, nothing will change.

I've been called in to companies after security breaches, only to find that backup systems existed—but the last clean copy was months old. Where MFA was "rolled out"—but only to executives, not the contractors with broad access. Where access controls were documented—yet dozens of former employees still had active credentials. None of these are problems with software or technology. They're governance problems. We don't need a new invention to fix them. We need leadership that treats cyber the way we treat fire codes.

To make matters worse, in most organizations the VPs and execs have all the authority but none of the responsibility. Many security officers at companies have been saying that better security measures are needed, but since they negatively impact the business, VPs choose not to implement the recommendations. When a hack occurs and data is compromised, instead of holding the VPs responsible, they fire the chief information security officer (CISO) who had been pursuing changes only to be ignored, and the problem never gets fixed.

When companies fail to secure their systems, it isn't just their reputation or quarterly earnings that take the hit. It's the trust of millions of customers whose personal data, health information, and financial stability can be stolen in seconds. It's the employees who lose paychecks when ransomware shuts down payroll systems. It's families who sit in dark homes when utilities are attacked.

Cybersecurity failures have a direct human cost. That's why the way we manage cyber risk inside organizations must evolve.

If we want true accountability and standardization, four changes to the cybersecurity practices of businesses are nonnegotiable:

1. CISOs Must Take a Risk-Based Approach

Too many organizations fall into the trap of trying to fix everything at once. But no business can eliminate every vulnerability. Systems are too complex, the attack surface is too large, and the threats evolve too quickly. That's why the best CISOs know they must prioritize changes based on what exposes the company to the largest amount of risk.

A risk-based approach means asking the following questions: "Which vulnerabilities would cause the most damage if exploited? Which systems are mission critical? Which data, if stolen, would create irreparable harm?" These are the areas where attention and resources must be focused first.

When companies fail to prioritize, they waste money patching low-level issues while leaving critical holes wide open. That's exactly what happened at Equifax—they ignored a known, high-priority vulnerability, and it cost them over $1 billion. For the average consumer, that meant a lifetime of credit monitoring and the permanent exposure of their identity. A risk-based approach doesn't just protect businesses—it protects every individual whose life is tied to that business.

2. Fix Root Causes, Not Just Symptoms

When a breach happens, many companies scramble to patch the hole that was exploited. They install new firewalls, roll out updates, or block a specific attack vector. But too often, they stop there. That's like treating a fever without looking for the infection causing it.

A symptom-based response leads to the same problems repeating again and again. If an employee fell for a phishing email, the solution isn't just another round of awareness training—it's examining why employees are so overwhelmed that they click in the first place, or why systems aren't segmented to limit damage when one person makes a mistake.

The root cause is almost always cultural: poor patch management, lack of clear accountability, or a focus on speed over security. Until leaders dig deeper, they're just playing whac-a-mole with hackers. And every time they miss, consumers lose.

3. Cybersecurity Must Drive Business Value

One of the biggest mistakes CISOs make is presenting security as a barrier. They say, "No, you can't launch that app," or "No, you can't roll out that new product." That kind of messaging turns cybersecurity into the enemy of innovation.

Yet cybersecurity done right drives business value. It builds customer trust. It protects intellectual property. It creates a competitive edge in markets where safety and reliability matter. The job of the CISO isn't to say no—it's to show that security enables the business to grow without fear. Think about it this way: Would you trust a bank that told you security slows them down, so they don't take it seriously? Of course not. Businesses that embrace security as part of their brand don't just protect their customers—they attract more of them.

4. Accountability Must Extend Beyond the CISO

This may be the hardest truth for organizations to accept: Security is not just the responsibility of the CISO or an equivalent role. That has to change. If a VP refuses to implement a critical security control, and that decision leads to a breach, they should be held accountable. In some cases, that means termination.

Just as a CFO would be fired for ignoring financial controls, executives who ignore cybersecurity controls must face real consequences. Without this standard, businesses will continue to treat security as optional—and consumers will continue to pay the price.

Cybersecurity is not just a technical issue—it's a leadership issue; it is a business issue. Until companies adopt a risk-based approach, address root causes, position cybersecurity as a business driver, and hold leaders accountable, breaches will remain the norm. And every breach means more stolen identities, more disrupted services, and more lives impacted.

If you take nothing else from this chapter, remember this: Leadership drives security. And whether you're a CISO in a Fortune 500 company, or a small business owner working on a laptop out of your kitchen, or someone who works from a desktop in an office every day, the responsibility is the same. Protect what matters most, make the hard decisions, and hold yourself—and those around you—accountable.

CYBERSECURITY IS NOT AN IT PROBLEM—IT'S A BUSINESS PROBLEM

One of the most dangerous misconceptions I continue to encounter in boardrooms or at an executive off-site is the belief that cybersecurity is a purely technical issue. I've sat across from CEOs, CFOs, and even general counsels who will nod gravely when a breach is mentioned and then immediately look toward the CIO or IT director as if to say, "That's your problem—fix it." This mindset is outdated, and frankly, it's reckless.

The idea that cybersecurity is nothing more than firewalls, antivirus software, or password resets misses the point entirely. Technology is only the tool; the real issue is how leaders manage risk, protect trust, and ensure the long-term survival of their organizations. When cybersecurity is pushed down to the IT department without executive ownership, the business is left blind to risks that can—and do—cripple companies overnight. It's like treating financial oversight as a bookkeeping function rather than a strategic driver of corporate stability. No board would allow the CFO to make decisions in a silo, but for some reason, many still believe the CISO should. That double standard has cost companies billions of dollars and destroyed careers, brands, and consumer confidence.

Cybersecurity today is inseparable from the health of the business itself. A successful attack doesn't just take down a server; it disrupts operations, halts revenue, and in some cases endangers lives. Think about hospitals that had to divert patients because ransomware locked their medical systems or pipelines that stopped fuel delivery across the East Coast after a single password compromise. These weren't "IT problems." They were business crises that impacted stock prices, consumer confidence, and even national security. If you're a retailer, a breach means customers walk away because they no longer trust you with their payment data. If you're a manufacturer, a ransomware attack means production lines grind to a halt, orders go unfilled, and your competitors seize market share. If you're in financial services, a cyberattack can erode confidence in your ability to safeguard wealth—a fatal blow for any bank or investment firm. The stakes aren't abstract. Cybersecurity failures directly affect earnings calls, investor relations, insurance costs, and regulatory exposure. In other words, every breach is ultimately measured in business outcomes, not just lost files.

And here's why you, the reader, need to understand this dynamic, even if you aren't a corporate executive: When businesses get cybersecurity wrong, it's consumers who pay the price. The Equifax breach wasn't just about corporate negligence—it was about nearly 150 million Americans whose Social Security numbers and personal histories were permanently exposed. When Target was hacked, the breach wasn't just a line item for shareholders—it was millions of families whose credit card details were stolen during the holiday shopping season. These failures remind us that cybersecurity is woven into the fabric of everyday life. Every time you swipe a card, log in to an app, or connect to Wi-Fi at a coffee shop, you're depending on businesses to have taken cybersecurity seriously. If they don't, you're the one left cleaning up the mess—freezing credit, replacing cards, disputing fraudulent charges, or worse, recovering from identity theft.

This is why I emphasize that cybersecurity is not just an IT issue and not just a business issue. It's a societal issue. For leaders, this means owning cybersecurity at the highest level of strategy. For individuals, it means recognizing that the digital health of the businesses you interact with has a direct impact on your personal safety. Until we shift our thinking at both levels, we'll keep repeating the same cycle: breaches, apologies, and broken trust.

If you doubt that cybersecurity is a business problem, look at the CEOs who had to testify before Congress after breaches. Look at companies whose market value dropped billions in hours after a hack was disclosed. Cybersecurity is not a side issue—it's a boardroom issue.

WHY BUSINESS CYBERSECURITY AFFECTS EVERYONE

The people most impacted by corporate cybersecurity failures are often the ones with the least power to do anything about it. In every major breach I've studied, the common denominator is this: Corporate neglect becomes consumer pain.

Think about how deeply businesses are intertwined with our personal lives. Your bank doesn't just hold your money—it holds your identity. Your hospital doesn't just store your medical history—it stores the intimate details of your life that you would never want exposed. Your favorite online store doesn't just sell you products—it processes your credit card, your shipping address, and your purchase patterns. Every one of those organizations is now a gatekeeper to your digital safety. And here's the harsh reality: You can't opt out. Most of us never asked Equifax to have our data; it was collected and stored without our direct consent. We didn't get to choose which subcontractors our utility company hired to manage billing software. We don't control which third-party vendors have access to the systems that run our schools, airports, or local governments. Yet every one of those points is a potential doorway for attackers. When companies fail at cybersecurity, they open the door to criminals—but it's you and I who walk through it, carrying the consequences for years to come.

This is why cybersecurity has to be reframed as a societal issue, not just a business issue. If companies are breached, it's not just an inconvenience; it can destabilize people's financial security, interrupt essential services, or even put lives at risk. When ransomware shut down the Colonial Pipeline, it wasn't the executives who were immediately affected—it was families on the East Coast lining up at gas stations, worried about getting to work or taking their kids to school. When health care systems are attacked, it's not the CIO who suffers first—it's the patients whose treatments are delayed and whose most private health records become bargaining chips for extortion. These examples underscore a simple but overlooked fact: The safety of our digital lives is directly linked to the security decisions businesses make. That's why executives must treat cybersecurity as a sacred trust. And it's why every individual, whether they realize it or not, has skin in the game when it comes to corporate cyber risk.

Think about it:

- If a retailer is hacked, your credit card information gets stolen.
- If a hospital's systems are locked by ransomware, your medical treatments could be delayed.
- If a school system is breached, your child's personal information could be sold on the dark web.
- If a utility company is attacked, your power, water, or internet could be disrupted.

When businesses ignore cybersecurity, they're not just risking their bottom line—they're exposing you.

EVERYDAY INTERACTIONS WITH TECHNOLOGY

You might think this is just about Fortune 500 companies. But let's bring it closer to home.

- *Smart homes*: Your thermostat, doorbell camera, and digital assistants all connect back to a company.

If that company cuts corners on cybersecurity, hackers don't just get into their servers—they may gain access to your home network, your cameras, even your daily routines.

- *Online shopping*: Every time you buy something, your data travels through payment processors, e-commerce platforms, and shipping systems. One weak link, and your card details are stolen.
- *Social media*: Businesses collect and store massive amounts of personal information. If they don't secure it, everything from your private messages to your family photos could be exposed.
- *Health care*: Hospitals and insurance companies now use AI to manage care and billing. That makes them more efficient—but also makes your health records a target for hackers.

This isn't abstract. Every click, swipe, and voice command ties you to businesses. And when those businesses fail at cybersecurity, you pay the price.

EVERYONE IS THE CEO OF THEIR OWN LIFE

The companies that take cybersecurity seriously aren't necessarily the ones with the most sophisticated technology—they're the ones where the CEO and board treat digital security as a core business risk. They don't outsource responsibility. They own it. They ask the hard questions: "What are our most valuable assets? What would happen if they were stolen or shut down? Are we investing enough to protect them?" And most importantly, they make decisions not just to save money today but to protect the company's future tomorrow. That leadership mindset is what separates organizations that survive a breach from those that collapse under the weight of one.

Now, here's the part most people miss: You need to apply the same mindset to your personal digital life. You may not run a global corporation, but you are absolutely the chief executive of your own data, your own finances, your own digital footprint. Every day, you interact with businesses and technologies that hold pieces of your life—your bank account, your medical history, your family photos, your identity. If a company you rely on is breached, it's your Social Security number or your child's information that gets sold on the dark web. And if you leave your accounts unprotected, it's your savings or reputation that's at risk. Just like a CEO can't afford to ignore risk management, you can't afford to assume that "it won't happen to me." In the digital age, every one of us is a target.

Being the CEO of your life doesn't mean becoming a cybersecurity expert or living in fear of technology. It means thinking strategically about your digital safety the same way a leader thinks about protecting a business. Start by asking yourself the questions great CEOs ask: "What are my most valuable assets?" (Is it your bank account, your credit, your health records?) "What would the damage look like if they were exposed? What simple steps can I take to protect them?" That might mean using a password manager, enabling two-factor authentication, freezing your credit, or being more intentional about what you share online. These are executive decisions for your digital life—investments in your own protection. And just like a business that takes cybersecurity seriously gains an advantage, individuals who adopt this mindset aren't just safer; they're freer to embrace technology with confidence instead of fear.

Think about how CEOs approach cybersecurity:

- They identify the most critical assets.
- They assess the risks.
- They invest in protection.
- They monitor and adapt as threats evolve.

That's exactly how you need to approach your personal cybersecurity. Because at the end of the day, while businesses have a responsibility to protect their customers, you can't outsource all your digital safety.

Being the CEO of your life means the following:

- Using strong passwords and two-factor authentication
- Monitoring your accounts and credit
- Being cautious with what you share online
- Demanding better cybersecurity from the businesses you trust with your data

If companies are failing to protect you, your responsibility is to protect yourself the way a business leader would—because in the digital age, that's the only way to survive and thrive.

THE COST OF IGNORANCE

Cybersecurity is overwhelming. It's complex, fast moving, and constantly changing. It's easy to feel powerless, to assume it's someone else's job—your IT department's, your government's, your software vendor's. But just as CEOs of Fortune 500 companies cannot ignore this problem anymore, we as CEOs of our own lives pay a steep cost for ignoring the problem as well. And the cost grows each year.

Let's break those costs down:

1. Personal Consequences

When cyberattacks hit individuals, they don't just drain accounts—they disrupt lives:

- *Identity theft*: With a stolen Social Security number and address, criminals can open credit card accounts, take out loans, and even commit crimes in your name. Victims often spend years cleaning up the mess, and some never fully recover their credit.
- *Financial ruin*: Retirement savings drained, college funds stolen, or mortgages compromised. These aren't hypotheticals—I've seen them firsthand. A grandmother in Virginia lost $60,000 she'd saved for her granddaughter's college after wiring money to someone she thought was a university administrator.
- *Reputation damage*: A deepfake video of you in a compromising position can ruin relationships and careers. Even if you prove it's fake, the stain often remains.
- *Emotional trauma*: Victims describe feeling violated, ashamed, and betrayed. I've met victims who blamed themselves for "not knowing better," though no reasonable person could have detected the AI-crafted scam that targeted them.

Here's a clear (and real) example from my work: A teacher clicked on what appeared to be a routine message from her principal. Within hours, her bank account was emptied, her email was compromised, and criminals had access to her student records.

The financial loss was recoverable; the emotional fallout was not. She told me, "It felt like someone had broken into my home and violated every part of my life."

2. Financial Consequences

For businesses, the costs are staggering. For families, they're devastating:

- *Small business collapse*: Many small businesses run on thin margins. A single fraud—like paying a fake invoice—can sink them. I consulted for a family-owned construction firm that lost $250,000 to a spoofed email "from a vendor." They closed within a year.
- *Health care ransomware*: Hospitals have paid millions in ransom, not just to restore data but to protect patients. In one German hospital, a ransomware attack forced a patient transfer that resulted in a death. The cost wasn't just financial—it was human life.
- *National-scale losses*: The Colonial Pipeline attack in 2021 showed how one breach could ripple across the economy. Gas shortages, panic buying, and millions in ransom highlighted how dependent modern life is on digital systems.

The average cost of a data breach in 2024 hit $4.88 million globally and nearly $10 million in the United States. That's just the direct costs—legal fees, settlements, forensic investigations. It doesn't include the hidden costs: lost productivity, lost customers, damaged reputation, staff turnover, stock price decline, lawsuits, and increased insurance premiums. And every year following is predicted to be an exponential increase in the frequency, impact, and damage.

3. Community Consequences

Communities often feel cyberattacks most acutely:

- *Schools*: When ransomware hits a district, children's personal data is exposed—addresses, health records, Social Security numbers. Some schools have had to cancel classes for days while IT systems were rebuilt. Or worse yet, when computers are given to schoolchildren, they can have malware installed that turns on the camera so children are monitored in their bedrooms when they are changing.
- *Local governments*: Baltimore was paralyzed in 2019 by a ransomware attack. City workers were locked out of email. Residents couldn't pay water bills or property taxes. Real estate transactions halted. The total financial cost? More than $18 million. Here's another example: In Texas, a school district was hit by ransomware that froze payroll. Teachers went weeks without pay. Morale plummeted, and several staff members left for other districts. The financial cost was heavy, but the community cost—lost trust between educators and administrators—was even greater.
- *Emergency services*: Several US counties have seen their 911 systems disrupted by cyberattacks. Dispatchers reverted to pen and paper. Ambulances were delayed. In moments when seconds matter, cyberattacks cost lives.

4. National and Global Consequences

At the national level, cyberattacks threaten infrastructure, stability, and even democracy itself:

- *Critical infrastructure*: Power grids, water treatment plants, and pipelines are all targets. In 2015, hackers shut down part of Ukraine's power grid, leaving hundreds of thousands without electricity. In 2021, hackers tried to poison a Florida water treatment plant by altering chemical levels.
- *Elections*: Deepfakes, disinformation campaigns, and hacked voter databases all undermine trust in democracy. Even when systems are secure, the perception of tampering can erode faith in election outcomes.
- *National security*: Breaches like the 2015 hack of the Office of Personnel Management (OPM)—which exposed personal details of twenty-one million US federal employees—hand adversaries intelligence that can be used for decades.

Globally, cyberattacks have become a tool of statecraft. They allow nations to disrupt rivals without firing a shot. The battlefield is invisible, but the damage is very real.

5. Societal Consequences: Trust on the Brink

Cyberattacks don't just steal data or money. They erode the very thing societies depend on—trust:

- When hospitals can't protect records, patients doubt their care.
- When schools can't keep data safe, parents doubt their administrators.
- When cities can't defend 911 systems, citizens doubt their leaders.
- When elections are clouded by disinformation, voters doubt democracy.

Even families feel this erosion. I've seen siblings go at each other after hacked accounts sent fraudulent messages. I've seen spouses blame one another after falling for scams. Cybercrime doesn't just target computers—it undermines relationships.

6. Generational Consequences

If we don't act, our children will inherit a digital world far more dangerous than ours.

Already, kids grow up sharing every detail of their lives online, often without realizing how permanent those footprints are. AI will only magnify the risks: deepfakes of teenagers created from social media clips, scams targeting young gamers, extortion based on stolen school records, etc.

Today's complacency becomes tomorrow's crisis. The digital traps we ignore now will ensnare our children later.

DISTINCTIONS BETWEEN HOME, WORK, AND PUBLIC DIGITAL USE

As CEOs of our own digital lives, it's important to recognize the different contexts where cybersecurity matters:

- *At home*: You rely on businesses to secure the apps, devices, and services that power your daily life. If they fail, your home becomes vulnerable.
- *At work*: Even if your company isn't a tech firm, it depends on digital infrastructure—email, payroll, client data. A breach at work doesn't just hurt the company—it can expose employee personal data, shut down salaries, or put jobs at risk.
- *In public*: From airports to coffee shops, we connect to public Wi-Fi and swipe cards through countless systems. Each one is a potential entry point for attackers if the underlying business doesn't take cybersecurity seriously.

No matter where you are, your digital safety is directly tied to how well businesses secure their systems.

AI: AMPLIFYING THE RISKS

So far, we've talked about cybersecurity in general. But let's add AI to the equation. AI is transforming business—making operations faster, smarter, and more automated. But it's also creating new risks:

- Attackers use AI to craft more convincing phishing emails, to automate hacking attempts, and to analyze stolen data at scale.
- Businesses use AI to process consumer data—but if that data is stolen, it's far richer and more dangerous than before.
- AI-powered decision-making (like credit scoring or

health care recommendations) can be manipulated if attackers tamper with the algorithms.

The danger is this: Businesses are rushing to deploy AI because it's profitable, but many are not securing it properly. And once again, that means the risk gets passed down to consumers.

FIGHTING THE INVISIBLE WAR

Cybersecurity is no longer optional. It's not just a technical issue—it's a human one, a societal one, and a generational one. Pretending it's "too complicated" or "someone else's problem" is no longer acceptable.

The invisible war is here. It's not fought with bullets but with data. Not with tanks but with algorithms. And the battlefield isn't overseas—it's in your pocket, your office, your school, your hospital.

Awareness is the first defense. Once you understand the threats, you can begin to defend against them. Once communities demand protection, governments move faster. Once businesses prioritize cybersecurity, they protect not only themselves but everyone they serve.

We don't need to be paralyzed by fear. But we do need to wake up. The cost of ignorance is too high.

FIVE CEO-STYLE MOVES TO PROTECT YOUR DIGITAL LIFE

1. Identify Your Critical Assets

A good CEO always knows what's most valuable. For a business, it might be trade secrets or customer data. For you, it's your financial accounts, Social Security number, medical records, and the devices you and your family use every day. Start by making a simple list of what's most important—and recognize that those are the prime targets for attackers.

2. Assess Your Risk Exposure

Companies run risk assessments to understand where they're vulnerable. You should too. Ask yourself, "Where do I store sensitive data? How many accounts do I have? Where am I reusing passwords? Where am I relying on companies I don't fully trust with my data?" Identifying weak spots is the first step to closing the gaps.

3. Invest in Protection

A CEO doesn't hesitate to spend money on security because they know the cost of a breach is far higher. Think the same way in your life. Buy a password manager, enable multi-factor authentication, freeze your credit, and keep your devices updated. A few small investments now can save you years of pain later.

4. Monitor and Respond Quickly

Just as companies use security operations centers to detect threats, you need to stay alert. Set up credit monitoring. Check your bank accounts weekly. Use alerts for logins and transactions. The faster you spot unusual activity, the less damage an attacker can do.

5. Lead with a Security Mindset

At the end of the day, leadership is about setting the tone. CEOs build a culture of security across their organizations—you should build one at home. Talk to your spouse, kids, or parents about safe online behavior. Treat your digital life like a business worth protecting, because it is.

When you think and act like the CEO of your digital life, you shift from being a passive target to an active defender. That mindset won't just keep you safe—it will give you the confidence to use technology without fear.

PERSONAL RESPONSIBILITY FOR THE DIGITAL AGE

Cybersecurity is no longer a technical issue that companies can push off to their IT departments—it's a core business risk that directly impacts every consumer. When businesses fail to protect their systems, it isn't just their bottom line that suffers; it's ordinary people whose data, finances, and daily lives are put at risk. The Equifax breach showed us that a single missed patch can expose half the country to identity theft. And as our world becomes increasingly digital—through smart homes, online shopping, health care systems, and now AI—the attack surface grows.

AI doesn't just create efficiency for business; it gives attackers smarter tools and richer targets. That's why cybersecurity must be treated as a boardroom issue, not an afterthought. For the average person, the lesson is clear: You can't rely on corporations alone to protect you. Just as a CEO safeguards the most valuable assets of a company, you must become the CEO of your own digital life—identifying your critical data, protecting it, and monitoring for threats. The digital age demands personal accountability, because when businesses stumble, the consequences land squarely on your doorstep.

KEY TAKEAWAYS

- ☐ Cybersecurity is a business problem, not just an IT problem. When businesses fail, consumers suffer.
- ☐ Everyday life is tied to business cybersecurity. From smart homes to hospitals, when companies are hacked, individuals are exposed.
- ☐ The costs are massive. Companies lose millions, but consumers pay with identity theft, fraud, and stress.
- ☐ AI raises the stakes. It accelerates both business operations and cyberattacks, creating new vulnerabilities.
- ☐ You are the CEO of your life. Protect your personal digital world with the same mindset that a CEO uses to protect a company.

CHAPTER 3

THE GLOBAL POLICY CHALLENGE

On a quiet Sunday morning in suburban Ohio, John Mitchell powered up his laptop using the same ritual he had followed for years. He made his coffee, settled at the kitchen table, and opened the accounting system for his small woodworking company. His business was simple: He built custom furniture, sold pieces online, and prided himself on old-fashioned craftsmanship in a high-tech world.

But this time, the familiar accounting dashboard never appeared. Instead, his screen filled with a pulsing black box. Crimson letters scrolled across the screen like something out of a dystopian movie:

"Your files have been encrypted. Pay $50,000 in Bitcoin in the next seventy-two hours or everything is gone. No payment = permanent deletion."

At first, John thought it must be some kind of scam pop-up. But when he tried to open his payroll records, his design files, even his customer emails, all of them were gibberish—long strings of nonsense characters, unreadable and locked away. He reached for his phone, heart pounding.

The local police officer who arrived at his shop was sympathetic but blunt: "This is cybercrime. It's not really something we can handle." He gave John a pamphlet with the FBI's website printed on it and left.

The FBI agent who eventually called back was even more direct.

"We know which group is behind this. They're based in Saint Petersburg, Russia. They've hit dozens of small businesses across the US. The problem is, they're beyond our reach. Russia doesn't extradite cybercriminals, and they won't cooperate with us."

Then, the FBI agent asked, "Do you have cyber insurance?" At that point John realized that his company, which he'd spent so many years building, was in jeopardy and that his life had now completely changed.

The agent didn't say the quiet part out loud: The hackers who had attacked John were operating in broad daylight, often tolerated—sometimes even encouraged—by their own government, as long as they never targeted fellow citizens. For John, the effect was devastating. He had employees to pay, customers waiting on orders, and tax filings due. Within weeks, his savings account was drained, his credit cards maxed out. His small dream of turning a woodworking hobby into a thriving business was teetering on collapse.

Meanwhile, in a café in Saint Petersburg, a young hacker leaned back in his chair, sipping coffee and laughing with friends. He wasn't worried about American law enforcement. He knew he was untouchable. This young hacker was an employee of a "legit" company in Russia whose entire business model and revenue were based on ransomware and extortion. Like a cyber version of the mafia, but operating remotely, able to access US companies as if they were blocks away.

This story may sound extreme, but it's not. It is the reality of cybercrime in the twenty-first century. Hackers can reach across oceans in milliseconds, paralyze lives and businesses, and face virtually no consequences. Borders mean nothing to them, but they mean everything to the people trying to stop them. John's story, unfortunately, is a regular occurrence that happens all across America and all around the world.

A GLOBAL PROBLEM WITHOUT BORDERS

John's story illustrates a painful truth: Cyber threats are not a local or even national issue. They are global, and no country or business is immune.

Consider just a handful of recent cases:

- A hospital system in Ireland shut down for weeks after a ransomware attack in 2021, forcing doctors to cancel surgeries and turn patients away.
- A Japanese video game company was hit, with hackers stealing sensitive customer data from millions of players worldwide.
- Law firms in London and New York were extorted, their confidential case files locked until ransom was paid.

What links these incidents is not geography, industry, or size. It is the borderless nature of digital crime. A hacker in Lagos can drain bank accounts in London. A coder in North Korea can launch phishing campaigns against teenagers in California. A group in Iran can disrupt a water treatment facility in Israel.

Traditional crime has physical limitations: Smuggling drugs requires border crossings, trafficking weapons requires shipments and logistics, and money laundering usually involves banks. Cybercrime has no such constraints. With a laptop, an internet connection, and a few hours of planning, a single individual can cause millions of dollars in damage across multiple continents.

Nuclear weapons can be controlled and sanctioned by international monitoring organizations like the UN and can be tracked with satellites. No such controls or regulations exist for perpetrating cybercrimes or creating digital weapons of mass destruction, yet the impact can be devastating. Companies like Iran and North Korea that are limited from having nuclear weapons are among the countries with the most devastating cyber weapons.

This raises a difficult question: How do you enforce the law when the crime scene exists everywhere and nowhere at the same time?

The answer, at least so far, is that we don't. Especially in the United States.

WHY THE LAW CAN'T CATCH UP

When cybercriminals strike, we often know who they are. Intelligence agencies track them, private companies publish detailed reports, and even journalists sometimes expose their identities. But knowing and prosecuting are two very different things.

The problem lies in jurisdiction. Law enforcement power stops at the border. To arrest someone in another country, the United States or any other nation needs cooperation from that government. That usually means an extradition treaty, a formal agreement that one country will hand over suspects to another. Just look at Edward Snowden. Because he went to Russia, he is untouchable. And he's a US citizen, so imagine trying to capture a Russian citizen.

Many of the worst cybercrime safe havens—Russia, China, Iran, North Korea—either do not have extradition treaties with the United States or deliberately refuse to honor them. Instead, they allow cybercriminals to operate freely, sometimes even offering quiet support if those criminals target the right enemies.

It's as if the world had agreed that murder, theft, and fraud were wrong but that certain countries carved out exceptions: "As long as you're only killing people in another country, feel free to do it here." Plus, in many countries, these criminals are even funded by the government or government officials are paid off, making it even impossible to take any action at all.

This legal vacuum explains why ransomware gangs continue to flourish, why stolen data circulates endlessly on dark markets, and why victims like John rarely see justice.

A PATCHWORK OF POLICIES

Governments have not stood still in the face of cybercrime. For more than two decades, leaders have introduced treaties, directives, and national laws meant to rein in the digital underworld. The problem is not a lack of effort but a lack of harmony. Instead of one clear playbook, the world has produced a patchwork quilt of policies—strong in some places, weak in others, and often incompatible across borders.

The Budapest Convention on Cybercrime, signed in 2001, remains the closest thing to a global treaty, with more than sixty nations agreeing to basic rules for investigation and cooperation. Yet Russia, China, and other major players refused to sign, leaving vast places for criminals to thrive. In Europe, the General Data Protection Regulation (GDPR) and NIS Directive set strict standards for privacy and infrastructure security, but their reach ends at the EU's borders. Asia shows promise, with nations like Singapore and Japan pushing strong national laws, while Africa has a continental framework on paper that many states still struggle to implement in practice.

The result is predictable: Criminals flock to the places where cybersecurity falls through the cracks, launching attacks from jurisdictions where enforcement is weak or nonexistent. Fragmentation, more than technology, has become the hacker's greatest ally.

As if cybersecurity weren't complicated enough, artificial intelligence has added a new layer. Governments are scrambling to regulate AI, but their approaches vary dramatically:

- In Europe, the newly adopted AI Act bans certain uses outright, such as social scoring, and imposes strict obligations on high-risk systems.
- In the United States, there is no comprehensive federal law. Agencies and states issue their own rules, leaving a fractured landscape.
- In China, the state requires AI systems to align with government ideology and has inserted monitoring mechanisms directly into platforms.
- In the United Kingdom, regulators favor a light-touch, sector-specific model, giving industries wide latitude.

This divergence creates confusion for businesses and opportunity for criminals. An AI system banned in Europe might thrive in a permissive jurisdiction, from where it can still target Europeans. Deepfake scams, automated hacking tools, and disinformation bots move freely across these regulatory seams.

THE GENERATIONAL GAP

Overlaying all this is a uniquely American problem: the generational gap in political leadership.

The average member of Congress is in their sixties. Many did not own a cell phone until they were well into adulthood. They came of age in a world without email, social media, or cloud computing. Asking them to legislate on ransomware, cryptocurrency laundering, or AI deepfakes is like asking a person who has never driven a car to write the rules of the road. The last two presidents of the United States were over eighty when they finished or will finish their terms.

Technology evolves exponentially. Policy evolves linearly. The gap between the two is growing, and it leaves citizens exposed.

POLICY SUCCESSES AND FAILURES

For all the frustration, it would be unfair to say that governments have made no progress. There have been genuine policy victories, moments when political will and public demand aligned to produce meaningful change. But there have also been glaring failures—times when leaders knew what needed to be done and still failed to act.

GDPR: Europe's Big Bang Moment

In 2018, the European Union did something bold. It passed the GDPR, a sweeping law that gave individuals unprecedented control over their personal information.

For decades, tech companies had treated personal data as free fuel. Every click, every photo, every purchase was collected, packaged, and sold with little oversight. GDPR flipped that script. It required companies to ask for consent, disclose how data would be used, and delete information upon request. It also came with teeth: fines up to 4 percent of global revenue.

The law sent shock waves around the world. American companies scrambled to update privacy policies. Asian firms built new compliance systems. For the first time, it wasn't Silicon Valley dictating the rules—it was Brussels.

Is GDPR perfect? No. Critics argue it is overly bureaucratic, difficult for small businesses, and unevenly enforced. But it accomplished something vital: It set a global benchmark. Even US states like California modeled their own privacy laws after it. Citizens everywhere became more aware of their rights.

GDPR proved that bold regulation was possible. It also proved that once one major region sets a standard, the rest of the world often follows. But the question remains: Why did the United States not adopt GDPR or come up with another set of laws? Over seven years later, Europe dominates privacy, while the United States has no unified federal laws, allowing threats to its citizens' privacy every single day.

The SEC's Cyber Disclosure Rule

In 2023, the US Securities and Exchange Commission quietly made history. It adopted a rule requiring publicly traded companies to disclose cyber incidents within four days of determining they were material—meaning they had a major impact on customers or the business.

Before this, companies often buried breaches for months, hoping the story would fade. Customers, investors, even employees were kept in the dark. The new rule changed that. Transparency became mandatory. If a company got hacked, the world had to know.

This was more than an accounting tweak. It was a cultural shift. Suddenly, CEOs and boards had to treat cybersecurity not as an IT problem but as a governance issue. Shareholders wanted answers. Regulators demanded accountability. Critics worried it might spook markets or tip off attackers. But the principle was sound: Sunlight is the best disinfectant. Companies that once hid their failures were now forced into the open.

Failures That Still Haunt Us

Yet for every success, there are failures that cast long shadows.

Take data privacy in the United States. Despite endless hearings, reports, and draft bills, the country still lacks a comprehensive federal privacy law. Instead, we have a patchwork of state laws—California, Virginia, Colorado, Utah—each with its own rules. For a company operating nationwide, it's a compliance nightmare. For citizens, it means your rights depend on your zip code.

Or consider ransomware. For years, governments have known exactly who runs the biggest gangs. Hacker groups like Conti, REvil, and LockBit are not mysteries. Intelligence reports have mapped their leaders, their servers, even their payment wallets. And yet most of these criminals continue to operate openly from safe havens. Some have been sanctioned, others indicted in absentia, but the majority remain untouched. Victims keep paying, and gangs keep evolving.

There are failures of imagination too. After the Colonial Pipeline attack in 2021, which caused gas shortages across the eastern United States, one might have expected a Manhattan Project–style mobilization. Instead, there were hearings, reports, and temporary task forces—but no systemic overhaul. The vulnerabilities remain, waiting for the next attack.

I was one of the few experts who accurately predicted that Colonial Pipeline was going to pay the ransomware as the only means of survival. Everyone doubted me, executives contradicted me, and the media wouldn't talk to me. Everyone thought that Colonial was going to be able to recover without paying the ransom. But the most economical solution was to pay the ransom. Once it was proven that I was correct, every media outlet wanted to talk with me.

Policy successes prove progress is possible. Policy failures remind us that progress is fragile, easily stalled by politics, bureaucracy, or inertia.

THE EVOLVING INTERNATIONAL POLICY AGENDA

Looking ahead, we see the international agenda shifting in two interwoven directions: AI regulation and cybersecurity cooperation.

AI: Between Promise and Peril

Artificial intelligence has become the darling of policymakers. Every nation wants to harness its promise—economic growth, medical breakthroughs, military advantages—while guarding against its perils.

The problem is that countries cannot agree on where the line should be drawn:

- *Europe leans toward caution*: The EU's AI Act categorizes systems by risk: minimal, limited, high, and unacceptable. High-risk systems, like those used in hiring or law enforcement, face strict requirements. Certain applications, like social scoring or emotion recognition in schools, are outright banned. Europe's message is clear: Human dignity and safety come before corporate convenience.
- *The United States favors innovation*: Policymakers worry that too much regulation will smother start-ups and cede ground to China. Instead of sweeping laws, the United States relies on agency guidance, voluntary frameworks, and a patchwork of state initiatives. The result is flexibility—but also fragmentation.
- *China treats AI as a tool of state power*: Regulations require AI systems to reflect socialist values and

often mandate "safety back doors" for government oversight. The goal is control, not freedom.
- *The United Kingdom positions itself as the "pragmatic middle"*: Its strategy is sector specific, relying on regulators in health care, finance, or education to set rules. The aim is agility, but the risk is inconsistency.

This divergence creates a regulatory maze. A company building an AI product must navigate conflicting requirements. A malicious actor can simply base operations in the weakest jurisdiction and reach across borders. Deepfake scams, algorithmic discrimination, and AI-driven propaganda don't stop at customs checkpoints.

In short, AI is global, but its governance is fractured.

Cybersecurity: Cooperation or Chaos

On the cybersecurity front, the international agenda is equally fraught. There are calls for the following:

- Stronger extradition treaties so cybercriminals can't hide behind borders
- International task forces, perhaps even a "Cyber Interpol," to coordinate real-time responses
- Norms of behavior, such as banning cyberattacks on hospitals or critical infrastructure, similar to the way chemical weapons are outlawed

But cooperation runs headlong into geopolitics. Russia and China resist Western frameworks, preferring to promote their own. The United Nations debates endlessly over definitions: Is state-sponsored hacking a crime or a national security prerogative? Is disinformation a weapon or free speech?

The result is paralysis. Everyone agrees that cybercrime is bad, but no one agrees on the rules.

WHAT CITIZENS CAN AND SHOULD EXPECT FROM THEIR LEADERS

Amid all this, one truth remains: The stakes are not abstract. They are personal. When a hospital's records are encrypted, it's not just a policy failure—someone's mother is missing surgery. When a law firm is hacked, it's not just a breach—a client's life is laid bare.

The evolving agenda will shape how safe—or unsafe—ordinary citizens feel in their daily lives. Whether leaders rise to the challenge will determine if cyberspace becomes more secure or more chaotic in the decade ahead.

Cybersecurity and AI may sound like distant, technical topics—things for specialists and committees. But for everyday citizens, these issues strike at the core of daily life: the security of your bank account, the privacy of your medical records, the reliability of your electricity, even the integrity of your democracy. Leaders who shrug off these responsibilities are not failing at the margins. They are failing at the foundation.

So what should citizens reasonably expect from those who hold power in an era where digital threats loom as large as physical ones?

Leaders Who Understand Technology at a Functional Level

No one expects members of Congress to write code or debug networks. But it is not too much to ask that lawmakers understand what ransomware is, how AI deepfakes can mislead voters, or why a data breach at a hospital can be life threatening. Too often, hearings in Washington reveal just how outdated the technical literacy of our leaders is. We've all cringed at viral clips of senators asking tech CEOs how the internet "makes money" or whether a smartphone can "listen to conversations without the battery installed."

This ignorance has real costs. Laws end up vague, outdated, or riddled with loopholes. Citizens should expect their leaders to invest in continuous learning—mandatory briefings, training programs, or even digital literacy tests for committee assignments. If a lawmaker wants to serve on a cybersecurity or AI oversight committee, they should prove at least a baseline understanding of the technology they're regulating.

Leaders Who Treat Cybersecurity as Nonpartisan

One of the gravest dangers in the United States is the tendency to turn everything into a partisan weapon. Cybersecurity cannot afford to become another casualty of political football. It should be treated like national defense, where disagreements may exist on strategy but not on the need for action.

Consider how Americans rallied after 9/11. The political climate was divided, yet both parties recognized that terrorism was a national threat. Funding, agencies, and reforms flowed quickly, sometimes even too quickly. Compare that urgency to the response after the Colonial Pipeline hack, when Americans literally lined up at gas stations in panic. Hearings were held, but meaningful bipartisan action fizzled.

Citizens should expect their representatives to put aside party talking points when it comes to protecting the digital backbone of the nation. The internet doesn't care if you're a Democrat or a Republican when it collapses.

Leaders Who Push for Global Cooperation

No nation can fight cybercrime alone. Just as climate change or pandemics demand global coordination, so too does cybersecurity. Citizens should demand leaders who are willing to sit at the international table—even with rivals—and hammer out agreements that protect everyone.

This doesn't mean naively trusting adversaries. It means acknowledging that certain norms, such as banning cyberattacks on hospitals or financial clearinghouses, are in everyone's interest. Citizens should hold leaders accountable for building coalitions, strengthening treaties, and refusing to let diplomatic inertia become an excuse.

Leaders Who Invest in Resilience

Cyber defense is not just about stopping every attack. That's impossible. It's about resilience—the ability to bounce back quickly when attacks happen. Citizens should expect leaders to fund modernization of critical infrastructure, support cyber education in schools, and create financial backstops for victims of large-scale attacks.

Think of it like public health. We don't just prevent disease; we build hospitals, train doctors, and stockpile medicine. Cyber resilience requires the same layered approach.

Leaders Who Communicate Honestly

Finally, citizens deserve transparency. When breaches occur, cover-ups only deepen mistrust. When policies are proposed, leaders should explain them in plain language, not bureaucratic jargon. Citizens should know when their data has been stolen, how it might be used, and what protections are being put in place.

Trust in government is already fragile. In the digital age, secrecy erodes it further. Honest communication can rebuild that bridge.

LESSONS FROM LEADERSHIP: FAILURES AND BRIGHT SPOTS

It helps to ground these expectations in real-world stories. Let's look at some leadership moments that reveal both what to avoid and what to emulate.

SolarWinds Breach

In late 2020, the world woke up to the scale of one of the most consequential cyber intrusions in history: the SolarWinds breach. Attackers—believed to be linked to a Russian intelligence service—inserted malicious code into a routine software update for SolarWinds' Orion platform, a tool widely used by US federal agencies and Fortune 500 companies to manage IT systems. When unsuspecting organizations installed the update, they effectively opened the door to the attackers, who gained stealthy access to sensitive networks. This wasn't a typical hack of one company; it was a compromise of the digital plumbing trusted by government and industry alike.

The scope was staggering. At least nine US federal agencies—including the Department of Homeland Security, the Treasury, and parts of the Pentagon—were infiltrated. The adversaries had months of undetected access, allowing them to move laterally across systems, monitor communications, and exfiltrate sensitive data. Unlike a smash-and-grab cybercrime, the SolarWinds attack was patient, strategic, and designed for long-term espionage. It revealed how a single weak link in the supply chain could cascade into a national security crisis, bypassing even well-defended systems.

What makes SolarWinds particularly troubling is that it demonstrated the asymmetry of cyber conflict. A highly resourced nation-state adversary was able to quietly compromise critical government systems through a single vendor, while defenders were left scrambling to understand the scale of the intrusion months after it occurred. It forced a reckoning inside government: Cybersecurity could no longer be treated as a patchwork of agency-level defenses but had to be understood as a systemic, nationwide challenge. The breach was not just a technical failure; it was a wake-up call that the digital supply chains underpinning government operations are as much a national security vulnerability as physical borders or military assets.

A separate and earlier hack highlights a different but equally alarming dimension of government vulnerability. The 2015 OPM hack, attributed to China, was a direct assault on sensitive government records. Hackers exfiltrated detailed personal files, fingerprints, and security clearance data on more than twenty-two million current and former federal employees. This was a treasure trove of intelligence that could be used to coerce, recruit, or track US officials for decades. The attack showed that the government's own aging systems and poor cyber hygiene could leave the identities and security of its workforce exposed.

SolarWinds in 2020, by contrast, was a supply chain

compromise that infiltrated government indirectly, through trusted private-sector technology. Instead of going after records stored in a single agency, attackers inserted malicious code into a software update used across multiple federal departments. Where OPM demonstrated the dangers of weak internal defenses, SolarWinds exposed the fragility of the government's reliance on external vendors. Together, the two breaches send a sobering message: Cyber adversaries don't need to storm the front gates when they can just as easily slip in through the back door. Whether through neglected legacy systems or corrupted supply chains, the result is the same—national security weakened from within.

Bright Spot: Estonia's Digital Resilience

Contrast these failures with Estonia, a small Baltic nation often overlooked on the world stage. In 2007, Estonia was hit by a massive cyberattack, widely attributed to Russia, that crippled banks, government websites, and media outlets. Instead of collapsing, Estonia treated the attack as a wake-up call.

The government invested heavily in cybersecurity, digitized its infrastructure with resilience in mind, and became a global leader in e-governance. Today, Estonia is one of the most secure digital nations in the world, often punching far above its weight in international cyber policy discussions.

The lesson is clear: Even small nations can lead if their leaders treat cyber threats as existential, not peripheral.

It's tempting to assume cybersecurity is the government's problem. But citizens are not just spectators; they are stakeholders. If leaders fail, ordinary people pay the price. Businesses close, bank accounts are drained, hospital surgeries are canceled, and elections are undermined.

Citizens should therefore not only expect action but demand it. Ask representatives what their cyber priorities are. Support candidates who treat technology seriously. Push back when leaders trivialize or politicize the issue. In the same way citizens once demanded environmental protections or consumer safety, they must now demand digital safety.

THE ROAD AHEAD

The global policy challenge is daunting, but it is not impossible. History reminds us that societies can rise to meet existential threats when they have the courage to act. After 9/11, governments rebuilt security systems in months. After the financial crash of 2008, nations coordinated unprecedented economic responses. Cybersecurity and AI demand that same level of urgency, because the stakes are just as high.

The road ahead will require three things above all: speed, vision, and accountability.

- *Speed, because technology evolves faster than legislation*: Leaders must accept that traditional timelines—years of debate, endless studies—are incompatible with the pace of digital threats.
- *Vision, because piecemeal fixes will not hold*: What is needed is a strategy that looks decades ahead, imagining not just today's attacks but tomorrow's. That means planning for quantum computing, autonomous weapons, and AI-driven misinformation wars.
- *Accountability, because without it, every failure repeats*: When a company loses millions of customer records, someone must be held responsible. When a

> nation fails to protect its citizens from ransomware gangs, leaders must answer for it. Accountability is not punishment—it is the only way progress sticks.

The future is not predetermined. Cyberspace can become either a secure foundation for prosperity or a lawless frontier ruled by criminals and hostile states. The difference will be whether leaders rise to the moment—or continue to treat technology as an afterthought.

Let's return to John Mitchell, the Ohio woodworker whose business was nearly destroyed by hackers. John was not a careless man. He installed antivirus software, updated his computer when prompted, and used strong passwords. Yet he still fell victim to an attack that originated thousands of miles away.

John's story is not about personal failure. It is about systemic failure. He was left vulnerable because international treaties don't align, because extradition agreements are ignored, because lawmakers bicker instead of legislate, and because too many leaders still treat technology as an afterthought.

When citizens like John lose everything, it should not be framed as an unfortunate accident. It should be seen for what it is: a betrayal of leadership.

And that is where citizens come in. Democracies respond to pressure. If voters demand action, leaders will move. If citizens stay silent, the inertia of politics will prevail. The digital future is not only in the hands of policymakers; it is also in the hands of the people who choose them.

So, the road ahead is not simply about treaties, regulations, or budgets. It is about a collective decision: Will we build a safer, smarter digital world, or will we stumble into chaos by neglect? The choice is ours, and the time to choose is now.

KEY TAKEAWAYS

- Leaders must demonstrate basic technical literacy. Citizens should not accept lawmakers who confuse apps with operating systems or who think AI is "magic." No one expects politicians to be engineers, but they should at least know the difference between a phishing email and a ransomware attack. Ignorance is no longer cute; it is dangerous.
- Cybersecurity must be treated as a nonpartisan priority. Imagine if Republicans and Democrats disagreed about whether the US Navy should exist. That is how absurd it is to politicize digital defense. Cyber threats target everyone. When a pipeline shuts down, both red and blue states run out of gas.
- Global cooperation is essential. Hackers don't stop at customs checkpoints, and malware doesn't need a passport. Unless nations work together—even with rivals—criminals will always have safe havens. The same way treaties once banned chemical weapons, the world now needs enforceable norms for cyberspace.
- Resilience matters as much as prevention. Attacks will get through. What matters is whether hospitals, banks, and power grids can recover quickly. Citizens should expect leaders to fund resilience the same way they fund highways or disaster relief. Think of cybersecurity not as a shield but as an immune system—strong, adaptive, and always ready.

- ☐ Transparency is nonnegotiable. Cover-ups breed distrust. When breaches happen, citizens deserve to know. When policies are proposed, people deserve explanations in plain language. Trust is the currency of democracy, and in the digital age, that currency is under constant strain. Leaders must protect it through honesty.

CHAPTER 4

SECURING YOUR SMARTPHONE

It started innocently enough. Maria was sitting in a coffee shop in Austin, Texas, scrolling through her phone while waiting for a client meeting. She received a text that appeared to be from her bank: "Suspicious activity detected on your account. Please verify immediately to avoid suspension."

Maria hesitated. She had just used her debit card that morning at a gas station, and something about the timing felt plausible. The message contained a link that looked almost identical to her bank's website. In a moment of rushed judgment, she tapped the link and entered her login details.

Within hours, $3,200 was drained from her account. The criminals didn't stop there—they used the same credentials to reset her email, access her cloud storage, and even impersonate her to her friends. By the time Maria realized the scope of what had happened, her entire digital identity was compromised.

The hardest part for her wasn't losing the money. It was the realization that the device she trusted the most—her smartphone, her constant companion—had become a weapon that had been used against her.

Maria's story is not rare. Every day, millions of people expose themselves to unnecessary risks through their phones. The danger isn't just theoretical—it's practical, personal, and devastating. Smartphones are powerful, but that power is a double-edged sword. If you don't secure them, they can be turned against you in ways you can't imagine.

HOW AI HAS TURNED SMARTPHONES INTO PRIME TARGETS

Maria's story of losing control of her phone is troubling enough on its own. But what makes the modern landscape even more dangerous is how artificial intelligence has supercharged the very threats aimed at smartphones.

In the past, text message scams were clumsy. Poor grammar, strange sender names, and generic messages gave them away. Today, AI writes flawless texts that read exactly like something your bank, your delivery service, or even your spouse might send. Criminals feed AI models your social media posts, location data, and browsing history. The result? Messages that feel eerily personal—custom tailored to trick you. Yes, with automation and scale, AI is creating customized attacks just for you and your family.

AI has also reshaped malware. Mobile malware once came from shady, obvious apps that few people downloaded. Now, attackers use AI to disguise rogue apps as legitimate ones, complete with fake reviews, logos, and descriptions generated by machines. These apps slide into app stores, harvest your contacts, track your movements, and sometimes record conversations—all while looking entirely normal.

Even voice and video aren't safe. AI can clone voices, making a scam call sound exactly like your child asking for urgent help. Deepfake video messages can impersonate coworkers or even executives at your company, urging you to install a "required update." On a small smartphone screen, where details are harder to scrutinize, these fakes are even more convincing.

And because smartphones are our constant companions—used for banking, payments, personal photos, and work—the payoff for attackers is enormous. One compromised phone can mean stolen money, leaked business data, or even identity theft across multiple accounts.

The takeaway is clear: AI hasn't just made smartphone threats more numerous. It has made them smarter, faster, and far harder to spot. The familiar red flags of yesterday's scams—typos, odd links, suspicious sender names—no longer apply. In today's AI-driven world, protecting your phone isn't optional. It's urgent.

THE MYTH OF BUILT-IN SECURITY

When you unbox a shiny new smartphone, it feels invincible. The sleek design, the fingerprint reader, the face unlock—everything gives the impression that your phone is a fortress. Apple and Google market their devices as "secure by design." While there's some truth in that, it's dangerously misleading.

Here's the reality: Your phone is not protecting you nearly as much as you think.

Yes, operating systems have built-in protections. iOS "sandboxes" apps so they can't easily talk to each other. (A sandbox is when each application is running in an isolated environment, so if one application gets compromised, it will not impact or compromise any other applications on the device.) Android has Google Play Protect to scan for malware. Both platforms release regular security updates. But these features are the equivalent of seat belts in a car—important but not foolproof. If you drive recklessly, ignore warning lights, or let strangers drive you around, that seat belt won't save you.

For example, if you download an app that requests excessive permissions—say, a flashlight app that wants access to your contacts and microphone—the phone's operating system won't stop you. It will politely ask if you want to grant access, and most people, eager to use the app, will tap "Allow." That's like handing a stranger the keys to your house because they promised to fix a light bulb.

The myth of built-in security lulls people into complacency. They assume, "If Apple let it into the App Store, it must be safe," or "If Android didn't flag it, I don't need to worry." This blind trust is exactly what attackers exploit.

Your smartphone is not secure by default. It is only as secure as the decisions you make.

THE FORBIDDEN F-WORD: FREE

Let's talk about one of the most dangerous four-letter words in the digital world: *free*.

Now, I grew up in New York, and I know the term *the F-word* usually means something else. But in cyberspace, *free* is the forbidden word you should fear the most. We love free. Free apps. Free games. Free photo editors. Free storage. The problem is, free is never truly free.

When you download a free app, you are paying—you just don't realize it. Instead of money, you're handing over your most valuable asset: your data.

Consider this: The majority of free apps demand access to things they don't actually need. Why does a free calculator app need your location? Why does a flashlight app need your microphone? It's not because they need those features to function. It's because your behavior, your location, your preferences, and your habits are being tracked, packaged, and sold.

At conferences, I often do a live demonstration. With permission, I'll grab someone's phone and open their location-tracking settings. Without fail, they are stunned to see dozens of apps quietly monitoring them: fitness apps, retail apps, even games they downloaded years ago and forgot about. I've had executives with multimillion-dollar companies sitting on stage, red faced with embarrassment, as they realize just how much of their life they've exposed for free.

So here's my challenge to you: Delete any app you haven't used in the last six months. I know it sounds like a lot of work. That's why I propose a simpler version: Delete one app a day. One app a day keeps evil away.

Think of it as a detox. In forty-five days, you'll have purged dozens of apps you don't use, dramatically reducing your exposure. This is one of the simplest, most effective steps you can take to secure your smartphone. And it costs nothing—except the courage to let go of the word *free*.

COMMON SMARTPHONE THREATS

Most people picture phone hacking as a Hollywood scene: a hoodie, a keyboard, and your screen melting. Real attackers are much lazier—and far more effective. They target the predictable places where humans take shortcuts: text messages, app permissions, backups, and account recovery. If you understand where the traps live, you'll stop stepping in them.

Malware on Mobile Is Real (and It Isn't Always Obvious)

Malware on smartphones rarely screams for attention. It whispers. A "system cleaner" quietly sends your contact list to a server in another country. A "battery optimizer" injects adware into your browser. A "document scanner" with AI bells and whistles uploads every PDF you ever scan—including your driver's license and tax forms.

Here's how this malware ends up on your phone:

- Sideloading on Android (installing apps from outside Google Play) is the front door for trojans. Most people don't wake up thinking, *I want to side-load malware today*. They click a link promising a premium feature for free, approve "Install unknown apps," and the damage is done.
- Enterprise or developer certificates can push unreviewed apps onto iPhones when users accept a profile from a link or a QR code. Once the profile is trusted, the phone will happily run whatever that profile tells it to run.
- Fake updates ("Your browser is out of date—tap here") trick users into installing malware. If an app or OS needs an update, it will update inside the App Store/Play Store or the system settings—never from a web pop-up.

What it looks like when you're infected:

- Battery drain that doesn't match your usage, unexplained data spikes, the microphone or camera indicator appearing without you initiating audio/video, or the browser's home page changing itself. None of these alone prove malware, but together they paint a picture you can't ignore.

Stalkerware and Spyware (the Abuse You Don't See Coming)

There's a nastier category of malware that isn't about money first—it's about control. Stalkerware markets itself as "child safety" or "employee monitoring," but in practice it gets installed by an abuser, jealous partner, or intrusive employer who wants your location, messages, and photos. On Android it often hides as a "system service." On iOS it's harder, but not impossible, via profiles, shared Apple IDs, or abused Family Sharing.

Here are some signs to watch for:

- You mention a location to no one, yet another person knows it. Bluetooth and Wi-Fi toggles change by themselves. Your iCloud/Google account shows new logins you don't recognize. If you suspect this, change your primary account password from a clean device, remove unknown devices from your account, review "Profiles/ Device Management" on iOS or "Device Admin apps/Accessibility" on Android, and consider a full factory reset.

Banking Trojans and "Overlay" Attacks

These types of malware are built to drain banking accounts. When you open a real banking app, the trojan displays a perfect fake login screen on top of it, captures your credentials, and passes you to the real app so nothing feels wrong. Later, the attackers pair your password with an intercepted SMS code (see SIM swap below) or social engineer the help desk to reset your MFA. Social engineering is when an attacker tricks someone into doing something they normally would not do. Since most people are trustworthy, social engineering is a very common tool to manipulate people into doing things that cause harm.

Credential Stuffing and Password Reuse

You didn't "get hacked." A different site did. Your reused password was sold for pennies, and attackers tried it against your email, cloud drive, and social media. One success opens the rest. On phones this often shows up as mysterious "new login" alerts; the real damage escalates when the attacker enrolls their own MFA device under your account.

SIM Swapping and Number Hijacking

Your phone number is the skeleton key to your life. Attackers use personal information about you that they gathered from other attacks to convince a phone carrier that the company is talking to you and not a hacker and that you bought a new phone and need to move your number to their SIM (or eSIM) to a new device. This means, essentially, that by convincing the phone company that they are you, they can switch your phone to their device, instantly hijacking your calls and texts (including two-factor authentication codes). Within minutes they intercept SMS logins and password resets. If your carrier offers it, enable a port-out/SIM-change PIN and ask for a "no-port" note on the line. On an iPhone, turn on eSIM Transfer Lock; on both platforms, prefer authenticator apps or hardware keys over SMS.

Smishing, Vishing, and QR-ishing

Text message phishing (smishing) is the most common consumer attack now because we trust our phones more than our laptops. Attackers mimic banks, toll agencies, shipping carriers, even your mobile provider. These scams follow a formula—what I call the UETA principle:

- *Urgency*: They demand immediate action before you have time to think.
- *Emotion*: They stir fear, anger, or shame to cloud your judgment.
- *Timely context*: They reference something plausible, like a recent trip or order.
- *Action required*: They push you to click a link or enter personal details.

Voice phishing (vishing) escalates by calling you "from" the bank's spoofed number to "verify" the fraud. A newer twist is QR-ishing—stickers placed on parking meters or menus where you expect a payment option, but the code instead leads you to a compromised site. You scan, you pay, and you pay the attacker.

Evil-Twin Wi-Fi and Captive-Portal Tricks

Your phone loves convenience. Auto-join Wi-Fi is a gift to attackers. They set up "Starbucks Wi-Fi" with a stronger signal than the real one, and your phone happily connects. Everything you do—especially to sites without HTTPS or inside apps with poor certificate pinning—can be intercepted or modified. Captive portals are also abused to push fake "security updates" for you to install.

Bluetooth, AirDrop, and Proximity Abuse

Short range doesn't mean safe. Misconfigured Bluetooth leaves doors open for data requests. AirDrop name and photo spoofing is used to drop malicious links or obscene images in crowded places. Keep AirDrop on "Contacts Only," and when you're not using Bluetooth in public, turn it off.

Cloud and Backup Exposures

End-to-end encryption in messages doesn't help if your cloud backups are unencrypted or accessible with your main account password. WhatsApp backups used to be a classic weak point; many people still have years of chats stored in recoverable form. Photo albums "shared with partner," cross-synced note apps, and shared drives leak more than malware ever could, because you consented to the leak.

Physical Threats That Become Digital

A thief doesn't need your phone; they need your passcode. Shoulder surfing your six-digit code at a bar and then grabbing the device is enough to change your Apple ID/Google password from the phone and lock you out of your digital life. This isn't theory—it's rampant. The defense is simple but uncomfortable: Use an alphanumeric passcode, turn on "Require Passcode Immediately," disable lock-screen changes (control center, wallet, USB accessories), and treat your passcode like your ATM PIN—shield it.

Supply Chain and Update Abuse

You trust the app. But can you trust every third-party library inside the app and every build system the developer uses? Attackers do "one-to-many" compromises by slipping malicious code into software updates. Your defense is boring but powerful: Limit the number of apps installed, favor reputable publishers with real security pages, and update promptly so you also receive security revocations when stores pull a malicious build.

Travel and Cross-Border Risk

Airports, conferences, and hotels are target rich—public charging stations with shady adapters, cloned "hotel Wi-Fi," and over-friendly "airport helpers" who offer to "install your airline app for you." If you frequently travel, consider a travel profile: a lean set of apps, minimal data, and a device you can wipe on return without losing your life.

BEST PRACTICES FOR SECURING SMARTPHONES

Think of this as a blueprint you can implement in layers—fifteen minutes for quick wins, sixty minutes for a full hardening pass, and a monthly tune-up to keep it tight. Everything below is pragmatic and field tested:

The Fifteen-Minute Baseline (Do This Now)

Start with the controls that close the biggest, easiest doors:

- *Update the OS and apps*: Open Settings → Software Update, then App Store/Play Store → Updates. Turn auto-updates on. This alone shuts down entire classes of exploits because many exploits take advantage of outdated operating systems and apps that have known vulnerabilities and have not been patched. When vendors find vulnerabilities in their software, they announce the vulnerability to the public along with a patch or a way to fix it. If you patch your systems in a timely manner, you are secure. However, if you wait, the attacker can break into your system before you patch it, using the known vulnerability.
- *Use a strong device lock*: Replace a four- or six-digit code with an alphanumeric passphrase you can type quickly (e.g., four real words with a separator). Keep Face ID/biometrics on for convenience, but make the fallback passcode strong. Set Auto-Lock to thirty to sixty seconds.
- *Lock what can change from the lock screen*: Disable access to Control Center, USB accessories, and Wallet/Payment when locked. Also block message previews while locked: Show Previews → When Unlocked. That stops shoulder surfers from harvesting 2FA codes.
- *Turn on Find My + remote wipe*: Ensure "Find My iPhone/Find My Device" is on and that "Erase after 10 failed passcode attempts" (iOS) or equivalent auto-reset (Android) is enabled. Verify you can sign into iCloud/Google from another device, and locate/wipe the phone in case it is stolen.
- *Check carrier protections*: Call your carrier and add a port-out/SIM-change PIN—a separate passcode

that must be provided before anyone can move your phone number to a new SIM card or account. This helps prevent the common scam called SIM swapping, described above. Ask if your carrier supports a no-port flag, which blocks all number transfers entirely unless you go in person and show ID. If you use an eSIM, enable eSIM Transfer Lock (on iOS) to stop attackers from digitally moving your eSIM to another phone. And no matter what, keep a paper copy of your recovery codes for critical accounts—so even if your phone is compromised, you can still get back in.

That's your first layer. You've just made yourself a very unappealing target because you have taken away all the common vectors that attackers use to compromise your device. The more you can think like a hacker and protect yourself, the more secure you will be.

The Sixty-Minute Hardening Pass (the Difference Maker)

Accounts and identity:

- Manage unique passwords for each account using a reputable password manager. On iPhone you can use iCloud Keychain; on Android use Google Password Manager or a third-party manager you trust. This is the rule: one account = one unique passphrase. If one site leaks, nothing else opens.
- Two-factor done right. Use an authenticator app (TOTP). TOTP is the standard behind most

authenticator apps (like Google Authenticator, Microsoft Authenticator, or Authy). TOTP works by generating a unique six- to eight-digit code on your phone that changes every thirty seconds. Because the code is calculated using both the current time and a secret key stored on your device, it can't be reused or guessed easily. Even if an attacker has your password, they'd also need access to your authenticator app at the exact moment to break in—making it far more secure than SMS codes.

- Or use hardware security keys (NFC/BLE like YubiKey) for banks, email, cloud, and password manager. These are physical devices you plug in or tap to prove your identity when logging in. Instead of typing in a code, you just touch or tap the hardware key to prove you're you. Because the cryptographic secrets never leave the device, it's much harder for attackers to phish or intercept than SMS or even app-based codes. These include the following:

    - NFC (Near Field Communication) lets the key authenticate wirelessly by holding it close to your phone, the same way Apple Pay or tap-to-pay credit cards work.
    - BLE (Bluetooth Low Energy) lets the key connect securely to your device over Bluetooth; useful for laptops, tablets, or phones without USB ports.
    - YubiKey is the best-known brand of these devices. It's a small USB-sized key that supports multiple connection types (USB, NFC, BLE)

and works with major services like Google, Microsoft, banks, and password managers.

- Use SMS only as a last resort. On iOS, you can store TOTP codes in the Passwords section for convenience; on Android, Google Authenticator/Microsoft Authenticator are fine—but back them up.
- Account recovery you control. Set recovery email/phone to numbers/emails only you control; remove ex-partners or old work emails. Add recovery contacts (for iPhone) and run Google Security Checkup (for Android) end to end.

Cloud and backups:

- On iPhone, enable Advanced Data Protection if you can handle the responsibility; it end-to-end encrypts most iCloud categories. On Android/Google, verify backup encryption, and review what's included—especially SMS if you still use it.
- Disable cloud backups for chats that you truly want end-to-end encrypted, or confirm they are now encrypted before enabling.

Permissions and privacy:

- Visit Privacy Dashboard (Android) or App Privacy Report (iOS). You'll see which apps use the camera, mic, location, photos, and contacts—and how often.

Anything that surprises you gets demoted or deleted.

- Set location to "While Using" for maps and ride-shares; never "Always" unless the app's core function is live tracking that you genuinely need. Many weather, shopping, and coupon apps quietly track "Always." Shut it down.
- Disable ad tracking (Limit Ad Personalization/Allow Apps to Request to Track → deny by default). You're not a product.

Browser and link safety:

- Use a mainstream browser with built-in safe browsing (Safari, Chrome, or Edge). Turn on fraudulent website warnings.
- Add a content blocker to reduce malvertising. Keep downloads off unless you absolutely need them. Never accept configuration profiles from random websites.

Messaging and calls:

- Default to end-to-end encrypted messengers with sane backups (iMessage, Signal, WhatsApp with encrypted backups enabled). For highly sensitive conversations, use Signal and verify safety numbers with the other person.
- Filter unknown senders (iOS: Settings → Messages → Filter Unknown Senders). Turn link previews off for unknowns. Do not tap shortened links; paste

them into a link expander or open from a desktop browser after inspection.

- For phone calls "from your bank," hang up and call the number on the back of your card. If they claim, "You'll lose your case if you disconnect," that's your confirmation that it's a scam.

Networks:

- Turn off Auto-Join for public networks. Use your personal hotspot instead. If you must use public Wi-Fi, use a reputable VPN you selected before you travel—not one offered by a captive portal.
- Disable Auto-Join Hotspot. Forget networks you no longer use. Enable Private Wi-Fi Address (iOS) / MAC randomization (Android) to make tracking you harder.

Bluetooth/AirDrop/NFC:

- Keep AirDrop = Contacts Only or Off. Disable NFC when you're not using tap-to-pay. Turn Bluetooth off in high-risk environments; if you need it for a watch or earbuds, at least review paired devices regularly and remove unknowns.

Payments:

- Remove Wallet from the lock screen. Require Face ID/biometrics for every transaction. Turn on transaction alerts for every card. Use virtual card numbers for online subscriptions when available.
- At restaurants and service counters, verify the amount from the notification before you leave. It takes five seconds and saves you real money.

Device hygiene:

- Delete one app per day for forty-five days. Less surface equals less risk. Ruthless is good here.
- Avoid rooting/jailbreaking apps unless you are intentionally accepting the risk. It's not "advanced"—it's "exposed."

These measures allow you to practice cybersecurity on a regular basis, so similar to brushing your teeth. They will help keep your device secure and much harder for an attacker to break in.

Monthly Tune-Up (Ten to Fifteen Minutes)

- *Updates*: OS and app updates, then a quick reboot. The reboot allows the changes to take effect. Many times, when you install a software update, the changes take effect only after a reboot.
- *Permissions audit*: Scan Privacy Dashboard/App

Privacy Report for surprises.

- *Account check*: Review new devices logged in to your Apple/Google account; remove anything unfamiliar.
- *Financial sweep*: Skim your card statements for small, repeating charges—those are the parasites that live forever if you let them.

Over the course of a month, small changes could cause vulnerabilities to become present on your device. These steps will make sure these vulnerabilities are reduced and that your device stays in a secure state.

High-Risk Mode (for Executives, Public Figures, or During Active Disputes)

This section outlines more advanced features for people who have a higher chance of being compromised. The reality, however, is that anyone can be targeted, so taking these steps on your device can also add that extra layer of security to make sure you do not become a victim:

- Enable Lockdown Mode (iOS) if you have credible targeted-attack risk; it disables high-risk features like certain message attachments and link previews.
- Use hardware security keys for email and cloud. This stops most credential-theft cascades cold.
- Carry a travel phone with minimal apps/data when crossing borders or attending large events. Assume it's compromised after the trip; wipe it and restore from a clean backup.

- Keep a written incident card in your wallet that includes the number to call to freeze your mobile line, your bank's fraud line, and the steps for remote wipe. In a real incident, clarity beats memory.

What to Do After Something Goes Wrong (Containment and Recovery)

Incidents happen. The winners aren't the people who never get attacked—the winners are the people who respond quickly and cleanly.

- *Isolate*: Put the phone in airplane mode (with Wi-Fi and Bluetooth off) and then using a second, clean device, decide what to do next.
- *Control accounts first*: Change your primary email/cloud passwords and revoke new devices. Rotate authenticator seeds only after you've secured email. Authenticator seeds are the hidden cryptographic secrets that power your authenticator app codes (TOTP). When you first set up two-factor authentication with an app like Google Authenticator, the service gives you a unique seed (often embedded in that QR code you scan). That seed is basically the "master key" your app uses—combined with the current time—to generate your rolling six-digit codes. If an attacker ever gets access to that seed (say, by breaching a cloud backup or tricking you into rescanning a QR code they control), they can generate the same codes on their own

device—effectively bypassing your second factor. That's why the guidance is this: Don't rotate or reset your authenticator seeds until you've secured your primary accounts (like email and cloud), or else you risk locking yourself out before attackers are blocked.

- *Notify bank/carrier*: Freeze the card, open a fraud case, add/confirm the carrier port-out PIN, and request a note that no changes can be made by phone.
- *Scan and reset*: On Android, run Play Protect and then back up essentials and factory reset. On iOS, if you suspect profiles/malware, go straight to Erase All Content and Settings, and restore only necessary apps from scratch—don't bring the parasite back with a blind restore.
- *Watch the blast radius*: If attackers touched your email, they touched everything your email can reset. Work outward: cloud, social, financial, and then anything with saved cards or rewards balances.

Coaching Your Family and Team (Because Your Risk Is Their Risk)

- *Kids/teens*: Turn on Screen Time/Family Link—not as punishment but as a safety net: app install approvals, location permissions "While Using," and purchase/subscribe prompts that go to a parent device. Teach them the UETA scam pattern (urgency, emotion, timely context, action required) and make "Show me before you tap" a family rule.

- *Spouse/parents*: Help them set a real passcode, review permissions, and put the bank and carrier fraud numbers in their contacts as favorites so they call the right number in a panic.
- *Work*: If your company allows personal devices for work, ask for a work profile (Android) or managed Apple ID with clear boundaries. You want security controls without giving the company access to your personal photos and messages.

THE MINDSET THAT ACTUALLY KEEPS YOU SAFE

Tools are necessary; mindset is decisive. When something pings you out of nowhere and demands a quick tap, assume it's hostile. When an app begs for permissions it doesn't truly need, assume it's nosy. When a public network looks helpful, assume it's not. You don't have to be paranoid—you just have to be procedural. Small, repeatable habits beat flashy security toys every day of the week.

And remember the challenge that always gets results with audiences: Delete one app a day for forty-five days. I've watched executives go from "My phone is a mess" to "My phone is a tool" in six weeks. Less noise, less surface, less risk.

If you implement only a fraction of what's above—updates on, strong passcode, carrier PIN, authenticator instead of SMS, locked lock-screen, lean app list—you've already moved yourself out of the "easy target" bucket. Attackers go where the doors are open. Your job is to close yours—consistently, without drama.

That is how you secure a smartphone in the real world.

KEY TAKEAWAYS

- ☐ Your phone is powerful but not invincible. Built-in protections are limited.
- ☐ Free apps are not free. If you aren't paying with money, you're paying with your data.
- ☐ Delete unused apps—start with one per day.
- ☐ The most common smartphone threats are malware, smishing, and rogue apps.
- ☐ Always update apps, read reviews, and check permissions.
- ☐ Watch for the UETA scam formula: urgency, emotion, timely context, action required.
- ☐ Secure your mobile payments with alerts, authentication, and awareness.
- ☐ Just as attackers use AI to trick you, you can use AI to filter scams, detect threats, and protect your finances—turning your smartphone into a more secure device.

BONUS TIPS: USING AI TO DEFEND YOUR SMARTPHONE

AI may make smartphone attacks faster, smarter, and harder to detect—but it also gives you powerful new tools to stay ahead. Just as criminals are weaponizing AI, you can use it as your ally.

AI-Powered Mobile Security Apps

Modern mobile security solutions don't just rely on virus definitions. They use AI to analyze behavior in real time. If an app suddenly starts transmitting unusual amounts of data, requesting risky permissions, or trying to run in the background constantly, AI can flag and block it before it causes damage.

Scam and Spam Filtering

Your phone carrier and messaging apps increasingly deploy AI to detect fraud. AI systems learn the patterns of smishing texts, robocalls, and spoofed messages, blocking them before you even see them. Turning on these filters is like having an always-on gatekeeper screening out the noise.

Smarter Fraud Detection in Payments

Apple Pay, Google Pay, and major banking apps now leverage AI to analyze your spending. If you normally buy coffee in Virginia and suddenly there's a charge in Europe, the AI notices instantly. These alerts give you the chance to shut down fraud before it spirals.

AI Identity Protection Tools

Some password managers and mobile identity apps now use AI to scan dark web markets, alerting you if your email or phone number shows up in a breach. They'll recommend stronger passwords or alert you to change a compromised credential before criminals exploit it.

Personal Security Coaching

AI "companions" are beginning to appear inside mobile operating systems—nudging you to review permissions, suggesting you uninstall apps you haven't used, and warning you about risky downloads. Think of it as a pocket-sized digital bodyguard that learns your habits and reminds you when you're slipping.

TOP FIVE AI TOOLS FOR SMARTPHONE SECURITY

AI-Powered Mobile Security Apps

Tools like Lookout, Norton Mobile Security, and Bitdefender Mobile use AI to detect malicious apps, spyware, and unsafe Wi-Fi in real time.

AI Scam and Spam Call Filters

AI-driven call protection (built into Android, iOS, and apps like Hiya) automatically blocks robocalls, fraud attempts, and suspicious texts before you even see them.

AI Phishing Detection in Messaging Apps

Platforms like Gmail, Outlook, and even Apple's Mail app leverage AI to catch suspicious links and scam messages sent via SMS or email.

AI Fraud Detection in Mobile Payments

Apple Pay, Google Pay, and most banking apps use AI to flag unusual payment activity and send instant alerts when something looks off.

AI-Powered Device Health Monitors

Some security suites and system tools now monitor your phone's behavior—flagging unusual battery drain, hidden processes, or data leaks that may indicate spyware.

CHAPTER 5

KEEPING COMPUTERS SECURE

Mark was a successful architect in Denver. He wasn't a "tech guy," but he considered himself reasonably savvy with technology. His office desktop was his lifeline—housing blueprints, contracts, billing records, and design software.

One late night, while reviewing project emails, he received a message that looked like it came from a popular file-sharing service. The subject line read, "Updated Client Contract—Urgent." Exhausted from a fourteen-hour day, Mark clicked the link without thinking twice.

The page asking him to sign in looked legitimate. He typed his credentials. Nothing happened. He shrugged, assuming it was a glitch, and went back to work.

By morning, chaos had erupted. His email had been hijacked. Fake invoices went out to his clients. Hackers had encrypted his project files, demanding $80,000 in cryptocurrency. Worse, his clients' personal information—including banking details—were leaked. His reputation, built over twenty years, was shattered overnight.

Mark's story is tragically common. One careless click can unravel a career, a business, or even a family's financial stability. And while smartphones dominate headlines, the computer—our trusted workhorse—remains the single most targeted and exploited device in cyberspace.

WHY COMPUTERS REMAIN A PRIME CYBER TARGET

Despite the rise of tablets and smartphones, computers are still the centerpiece of modern life. Businesses run on them. Students rely on them for school. Families use them for banking, shopping, and storing memories. That makes them irresistible to attackers.

Why are computers—laptops and desktops—still consistently targets of cyberattacks? For these five reasons:

1. Bigger Attack Surface

Computers hold more data than phones: years of emails, financial records, tax filings, contracts, photos, and saved logins. To an attacker, this is a treasure chest.

2. Legacy Software and Systems

Unlike phones, which force updates more aggressively, computers often run outdated software. Some businesses still use Windows 7 or old versions of Office. Attackers thrive on these outdated models. Every outdated system is a welcome mat.

3. More Complex and Easier to Exploit

An operating system running on a computer is much more complex, has more vulnerabilities, and has more ways for an attacker to break in and go unnoticed. Many of the exploits run by attackers today will only work on a computer. The attacks can't run on a smartphone or tablet because those are much simpler systems and therefore harder to exploit.

4. Gateway to Networks

A compromised computer doesn't just impact the user—it can open the door to an entire office network. That's why ransomware groups target desktops first: Compromise one, spread laterally, and then cripple the whole organization.

5. Human Habits

Computers are where most people check email, download files, and click links. This makes them the front line for phishing attacks. Humans—not machines—are the weakest link, and computers are where those weaknesses are exploited most.

Computers remain prime targets because they sit at the crossroads of data, networks, and human behavior. Attackers know this. That's why you must know it too—and protect yourself.

HOW AI SUPERCHARGES ATTACKS AND RAISES THE STAKES

Mark's story highlights how one tired moment can unravel years of work. But there's a deeper problem: The attacker on the other side of that email wasn't even working alone. Increasingly, they're being assisted—or entirely replaced—by artificial intelligence. Today, AI writes flawless emails that mimic the tone, vocabulary, and even the urgency of a real colleague. The fake contract Mark received could have been generated by an AI system trained on thousands of legitimate legal documents, making it indistinguishable from the real thing.

And it doesn't stop with email. AI is being used to do the following:

- *Automate attacks at scale*: Instead of manually sending a few hundred phishing emails, AI can craft and personalize thousands every minute. Each message feels authentic because it can pull from publicly available data about you, your company, and your habits.
- *Bypass security tools*: AI-driven malware constantly mutates its code so that traditional antivirus software doesn't recognize it. Imagine a virus that changes its appearance every time you look at it—AI makes that transformation possible.
- *Exploit human psychology*: AI analyzes patterns in human behavior and tailors attacks to your exact vulnerabilities. If you tend to open emails late at night, it times them to arrive when you're most tired. If you've been posting about travel on social media, it sends fake airline updates to your inbox.
- *Generate deepfakes and synthetic voices*: It's no longer just an email risk. Attackers can now create a voice message that sounds exactly like your boss, urging you to "approve the urgent wire transfer" or "reset your credentials."

The result is chilling: The barrier to entry for cybercrime has dropped. What once required technical expertise can now be done by anyone with an AI tool kit purchased on the dark web. That means more attacks, more convincing scams, and far less room for error on the part of everyday users.

This is why computers remain at the center of the storm. They are the hub of your professional and financial life—and they're exactly where AI-enhanced attacks are aimed. The sobering truth is that no one is "too smart" to fall for these traps anymore. The game has shifted. The question isn't whether hackers are targeting you—it's whether you've built enough layers of defense to withstand the attack when it inevitably comes.

BASIC AND ADVANCED COMPUTER SECURITY TIPS

Securing your computer doesn't mean you have to become a tech wizard. It means following disciplined, layered habits that shrink your attack surface. Think of it like locking your doors, setting an alarm, and checking your windows. One lock isn't enough—you need layers.

Basic Habits (the Nonnegotiables)

Keep Your Operating System Updated

Updates are not annoyances—they are shields. Every Tuesday, sometimes called "Patch Tuesday," companies like Microsoft and Apple release fixes for vulnerabilities. Attackers reverse engineer those patches within days to exploit anyone who delays. The rule: Install updates immediately.

Strong Passwords + Multi-Factor Authentication

If your computer account is protected by "Password123," you're already compromised. Use a long, unique passphrase (think "FourRandomWords!2024"). Add MFA wherever possible—particularly for email and banking.

Lock Your Screen

It sounds basic, but some breaches happen physically. People at the airport or coffee shop walk away from their computer for three to five minutes, and someone either installs malware, accesses their account, or steals their computer. Many people are trustworthy and think they can walk away from their computer and it will be safe, but attackers target coffee shops, hotels, and airports waiting to take advantage or accessing an unattended device. Always lock your screen when stepping away. On Windows: Windows + L. On Mac: Control + Command + Q.

Back Up Your Data

Ransomware loses its sting if you have clean backups. Use a combination of cloud storage (with encryption) and an external hard drive. Test your backups—don't just assume they work. Ransomware works by encrypting all your files and demanding payment for the decryption key. The attacker's leverage is simple: If you can't access your data, your business grinds to a halt. But that power only holds if you don't have another way to get your files back. If you maintain clean, isolated backups—copies of your data that the ransomware can't touch—you can wipe the infected machines and restore everything without paying a dime. In other words, backups neutralize the attacker's main weapon: the threat of permanent data loss. That's why "clean" is so important. If your backups are connected to the network during the attack or haven't been tested, they may be encrypted too, leaving you no better off. A layered approach—using encrypted cloud storage and a disconnected external drive and regularly testing recovery—ensures that when ransomware strikes, it's a nuisance, not a catastrophe.

Advanced Habits (for Those Ready to Level Up)

Use a Standard User Account for Daily Work

On Windows, don't run everything as "Administrator." Create a standard account for daily tasks. This prevents malware from automatically gaining system-wide control.

Enable Disk Encryption

Both Windows (BitLocker) and Mac (FileVault) offer full-disk encryption. If your laptop is stolen, encryption ensures that thieves can't access your files without your password.

Consider Virtual Machines or Sandboxes

If you frequently test software or download files, use a virtual machine (VM) or sandbox environment. That way, if malware slips in, it's contained. A VM is like a computer inside your computer. It runs as software but acts like a separate system with its own operating system, files, and applications. Because it's isolated from your main system, anything you do inside the VM—whether testing new software or opening a suspicious file—stays contained. If malware infects the VM, it doesn't automatically spill over into your actual computer. You can simply reset or delete the VM and start fresh.

A sandbox environment is a lighter-weight version of that same idea. Instead of running a full second operating system, a sandbox is a controlled, restricted space where you can open files or run programs without giving them full access to your machine. Think of it as a quarantine zone: The software can run, but it's walled off from your critical data and settings. If it turns out to be malicious, the damage is contained to the sandbox, which you can discard safely.

Use Hardware Security Keys

For critical accounts, hardware keys like YubiKey offer protection that SMS codes can't. Even if your password is stolen, attackers can't log in without the physical key.

Hardware security keys like YubiKey raise the bar because they require something you physically possess—not just something you know or something sent to your phone. SMS codes can be intercepted through SIM swapping, phishing, or by attackers who compromise the phone network itself. A YubiKey, by contrast, plugs into your computer or taps wirelessly against your phone (via NFC/Bluetooth) to prove your identity using cryptography. The private key never leaves the device, so even if a hacker tricks you into visiting a fake login page, they can't copy or replay the hardware response. This means that an attacker on the other side of the world, even with your username and password in hand, hits a dead end if they don't also have the tiny physical key in their pocket.

A striking example comes from Google. After years of battling phishing attacks against its employees, the company rolled out YubiKeys across its workforce. The results were dramatic: Successful phishing attempts dropped to zero. By requiring a physical key for login, Google removed the attackers' ability to exploit stolen passwords or trick employees with fake login pages. That success story illustrates the power of hardware keys—not just as a stronger form of two-factor authentication but as a game-changing defense against one of the most common attack vectors on the planet.

Monitor Your System Logs

Advanced users can review firewall and system logs for suspicious activity. Unexpected traffic, repeated login attempts, or unusual processes can signal compromise. For an individual, reviewing firewall and system logs doesn't have to mean wading through endless lines of code. Most home routers and security software include a dashboard where you can view recent activity. Start by logging in to your router and checking for unfamiliar devices connected to your network—if you see a laptop, phone, or smart device you don't recognize, that's a red flag. On your computer, both Windows and macOS have built-in tools (like Windows Event Viewer or macOS Console) that let you search for repeated failed login attempts or unusual applications trying to run. Many personal firewalls and antivirus programs simplify this by flagging suspicious traffic—such as repeated connections to strange IP addresses in foreign countries. Even just checking once a month, or after you notice your system acting slow or odd, can help you catch early signs of compromise. And if you're not comfortable digging into the raw logs, there are user-friendly tools and apps (such as Little Snitch on Mac or GlassWire on Windows) that visualize traffic and highlight anomalies in plain English.

Basic or advanced, the principle is the same: Build habits that make you a harder target. Attackers prefer low-hanging fruit. Don't be the fruit.

SAFE DOWNLOAD PRACTICES—ANTIVIRUS AND SAFE SOURCES

Downloads are the number one way malware sneaks into computers. It doesn't matter if you're downloading movies, software, or PDFs—if the source is shady, the risk is real.

Antivirus Is Necessary but Not Sufficient

You should run antivirus. Windows Defender (built into Windows 10 and 11) and macOS XProtect (built into every Mac) are the operating systems' native security tools. They automatically scan files, monitor downloads, and block known malware without you needing to install anything extra. Both have improved dramatically in recent years, updating in the background with new threat intelligence from Microsoft and Apple. But they're not magic shields—these tools mainly catch known threats and basic attacks. They can't always stop brand-new malware, phishing attempts, or clever social engineering. That's why you still need good habits on top of antivirus: keeping systems patched, using strong passwords, and being cautious about what you click.

Antivirus should be seen as one layer—not the only layer. Attackers constantly develop new malware that can slip past detection.

RULES FOR SAFE DOWNLOADS

Use Official Sources Only

Download software from the vendor's official site or a trusted app store. Never trust third-party "download sites" filled with pop-ups and ads.

Verify Digital Signatures

Many programs are signed by the developer. On Windows or macOS, you can check the digital certificate before installing. If it doesn't match, don't install.

Be Wary of "Free" Software

Remember the forbidden *F-word: free*. Free software often bundles spyware or adware. If you need free tools, stick to reputable open-source projects.

Scan Before Opening

Right-click a file and scan it with your antivirus before opening. If it's an email attachment, be doubly cautious.

Avoid Pirated Software

Pirated programs are malware delivery systems disguised as bargains. That "free" Photoshop download can cost you thousands in stolen data.

RECOGNIZING PHISHING EMAILS AND SUSPICIOUS ATTACHMENTS

Email is the hacker's favorite weapon. Why? Because it works. Phishing preys on psychology: urgency, fear, greed, or curiosity.

Red Flags of a Phishing Email

How do you know if an email is a scam? There are typically five things to look out for—a twist on the UETA principle:

- *Urgency*: "Act now or lose access."
- *Emotion*: "Your account will be suspended."
- *Suspicious sender*: An address that looks close to the real thing but isn't exact (e.g., support@paypa1.com).
- *Attachments you weren't expecting*: Even if it looks like an invoice, pause.
- *Generic greetings*: "Dear Customer" instead of your name.

Real-World Example: The Résumé Scam

A midsize law firm once received dozens of emails with attachments labeled "Résumé.pdf." At first, the messages blended in with normal HR traffic—after all, law firms often advertise openings and regularly receive candidate résumés. What raised suspicion was volume: The number of applications suddenly spiked, and IT staff noticed that the attachments were unusually large for simple text-based résumés. When one was opened in a test environment, it triggered unexpected network connections to an external server—classic malware behavior.

The impact was immediate. The malware installed remote access tools that gave attackers a foothold inside the firm's network. From there, the attackers began scanning internal systems and exfiltrating sensitive case files. Had this gone unnoticed longer, client confidentiality could have been destroyed and the firm's reputation severely damaged. Fortunately, because IT caught the anomaly early, they were able to limit the spread before major legal data was compromised.

Cleanup required a full-scale incident response. The firm's IT team isolated the infected machines, blocked malicious IP addresses, and restored clean versions of the systems from backups. They also reset all user credentials, applied updated spam filters to block similar attachments, and trained HR staff to handle résumés more safely by opening them only in a sandbox or virtual machine. The lesson was clear: Even something as mundane as a job application can be weaponized, and without vigilance, an innocent-looking attachment can hand over the keys to an entire network.

How to Respond

- Don't click links in suspicious emails. Type the URL address manually into your browser.
- Don't open attachments unless you're expecting them. Call the sender to verify.
- Use email filters and advanced threat protection if available.

Lessons Learned: How to Avoid the Résumé Scam

- Verify attachments before opening: Treat unexpected résumés, invoices, or documents as suspicious—especially if they come in bulk or from unknown senders.
- Use a sandbox or VM: Open résumés and other attachments in a contained environment so malware can't reach your main system.
- Train staff, not just IT: HR, finance, and admin teams are prime targets—make sure they know how to spot phishing and handle files safely.
- Monitor for unusual activity: Spikes in email volume, large attachments, or unexpected outbound network traffic should trigger investigation.
- Back up and prepare: Clean backups and a practiced incident response plan make recovery faster and less damaging if something slips through.

SECURING FINANCIAL INFORMATION AND ACCOUNTS

Few things are more terrifying than logging in to your bank and seeing money missing. Financial accounts are prime targets, but you can protect them.

Dedicated Computer for Finances

If possible, use a separate device (or at least a separate user account) for financial activity. Don't mix banking with web surfing and gaming.

Alerts on Every Transaction

Set up text or app notifications for charges. Yes, it's a minor inconvenience—but catching fraud early saves far greater pain later.

Virtual Card Numbers

Many banks now offer disposable card numbers for online purchases. If the number is stolen, it can't be reused.

Secure Your Wi-Fi

Never bank over public Wi-Fi. Public hotspots at airports, hotels, or coffee shops are often unencrypted, which means attackers can sit on the same network and intercept your traffic, stealing logins or injecting malware. At home, use WPA3 encryption—the latest Wi-Fi security standard that makes it far harder for outsiders to crack your network. Always set a strong, unique router password and replace the default login credentials, since those are widely published online and often the first thing attackers try. Changing these settings ensures your home network isn't running on "factory defaults" that criminals already know how to exploit.

Two-Factor Authentication

Always enable it for financial accounts. Use authenticator apps or hardware keys instead of SMS where possible. This means you need not only your password but also a second proof of identity when logging in. The safest options are authenticator apps (which generate time-based one-time codes, like Google Authenticator, Microsoft Authenticator, or Authy) or hardware security keys (physical devices like YubiKey). These methods are far stronger than SMS codes, which attackers can intercept through SIM swapping or by compromising the phone network. By requiring either a code that changes every thirty seconds or a physical key in your hand, you make it virtually impossible for someone to break into your bank, credit card, or investment accounts—even if they steal your password.

Monitor Credit Reports

In the United States, you can check your credit reports for free annually. Services like Credit Karma also help monitor activity. Freeze your credit if you're not actively using it.

USING AI AS YOUR CYBERSECURITY ALLY

AI may give attackers new weapons, but it also arms defenders with tools we've never had before. The same intelligence that criminals exploit can be harnessed by everyday users to stay safer, spot threats earlier, and respond faster. The key is not to fear AI but to put it to work on your side.

Smarter Threat Detection

Modern antivirus and endpoint protection systems use AI to recognize unusual behavior, not just known signatures. That means your security tools can flag a program that is acting suspiciously, even if it's brand-new malware the world has never seen.

Real-Time Phishing Filters

Email providers now deploy AI models to scan billions of messages and catch subtle cues that even sharp-eyed users might miss. AI can spot impersonation patterns, malicious links, and deepfake attachments before they ever reach your inbox.

Password and Identity Management

AI-powered password managers can analyze your credentials, flag weak or reused ones, and even generate stronger passphrases tailored to meet modern complexity standards. Some can predict which of your accounts are most at risk based on real-world breach data.

Fraud and Financial Alerts

Banks and credit card companies use AI to detect unusual activity—whether that's a two-dollar test charge in another country or a sudden string of logins from multiple locations. These alerts give you a chance to shut down fraud before it snowballs.

Personalized Security Coaching

Some tools now act as AI "copilots," analyzing your behavior and recommending safer habits: reminding you to update, warning you about risky downloads, or suggesting when it's time to rotate a password. Think of it as a digital security coach sitting quietly on your shoulder.

Automated Response

If a breach occurs, AI can help contain it faster by isolating infected files, locking suspicious accounts, and guiding you step-by-step through recovery. What once took hours of panic can now be reduced to minutes of controlled action.

In the wrong hands, AI makes attacks faster and smarter. In your hands, it can be the watchdog that never sleeps, scanning, learning, and defending around the clock. The challenge is not whether AI will shape the future of cybersecurity—it already has. The challenge is whether you will use it as a shield or allow attackers to use it as a sword.

TOP FIVE AI TOOLS YOU SHOULD ENABLE TO PROTECT YOUR COMPUTER TODAY

AI-Powered Antivirus/Endpoint Protection

Modern tools use AI to detect suspicious behavior, not just old virus signatures. Examples include Windows Defender with cloud-based protection, CrowdStrike Falcon, or Bitdefender.

AI Email Filters

Services like Microsoft 365, Gmail, and Proofpoint deploy AI to catch phishing and deepfake-laced messages before they reach your inbox. Turn these filters on—and don't override them.

AI-Driven Password Managers

Tools like 1Password or Dashlane flag weak or reused passwords and suggest stronger ones, powered by AI analysis of real-world breaches.

AI Fraud Detection in Banking

Most major banks use AI to monitor your spending patterns. Enable transaction alerts so you get notified when the system spots unusual activity.

Personal AI Security Assistants

Some platforms now act as "cyber copilots," reminding you to update, flagging risky downloads, and helping you respond to incidents faster. Treat them like a digital coach.

KEY TAKEAWAYS

- ☐ Keeping computers secure is about discipline, not paranoia.
- ☐ Computers remain prime targets because of the data they hold and the habits of their users.
- ☐ Basic security—updates, strong passwords, backups—blocks most attacks.
- ☐ Advanced security—disk encryption, hardware keys, sandboxing—raises the bar even higher.
- ☐ Safe download practices are essential: official sources only, no pirated software.
- ☐ Phishing emails are the number one way people are compromised—learn the red flags.
- ☐ Protect financial accounts with alerts, two-factor authentication, and secure networks.
- ☐ Security is not about being perfect. It's about being prepared, disciplined, and one step harder to hack than the next target.

FINAL CHECKLIST: TOP TEN HABITS FOR SECURE COMPUTING

- ☐ *Update immediately*: Install OS and app updates as soon as they're released.
- ☐ *Use strong passphrases*: Make every account unique and hard to guess.
- ☐ *Turn on MFA*: Add multi-factor authentication wherever possible.
- ☐ *Lock your screen*: Always lock when stepping away (Windows + L or Control + Command + Q).
- ☐ *Back up twice*: One cloud backup, one external drive. Test them regularly.
- ☐ *Encrypt your drive*: Turn on BitLocker (Windows) or FileVault (Mac).
- ☐ *Download wisely*: Stick to official sources, never pirated software.
- ☐ *Spot phishing*: Watch for urgency, fear, generic greetings, and odd links.
- ☐ *Protect finances*: Set alerts on every transaction; use virtual cards online.
- ☐ *Audit monthly*: Review accounts, devices, and app permissions for surprises.

CHAPTER 6

CLOUD SECURITY ESSENTIALS

Jasmine was a freelance photographer in Chicago. She loved the cloud because it gave her freedom. No bulky hard drives, no worrying about losing her laptop—everything she needed lived in her Dropbox and Google Drive accounts: contracts, tax forms, wedding photos, client galleries. It was all there, accessible from anywhere.

One morning she logged in to share a gallery with a client, only to find her folders gone. At first, she thought it was a glitch. Then she saw the email: "We have your files. Pay $10,000 in Bitcoin within seventy-two hours or everything will be deleted."

She froze. These weren't just pictures. Some files contained sensitive client information, including scanned IDs for destination weddings. Her entire business reputation—and her clients' trust—was on the line. Jasmine hadn't enabled two-factor authentication, hadn't used unique passwords, and had been logging in to public Wi-Fi networks without a VPN.

The hackers didn't need to breach Dropbox or Google. They only needed her weak habits. And they used them to hold her livelihood hostage.

WHAT THE CLOUD ACTUALLY MEANS FOR YOUR DATA

We toss around the term *cloud* like it's some mysterious place in the sky. In reality, the cloud is just someone else's computer—giant data centers owned by companies like Google, Microsoft, Apple, or Amazon.

When you upload a file to Google Drive, iCloud, or Dropbox, that file is stored on servers in a secure facility. You access it through the internet instead of a local hard drive. This setup gives you flexibility: Your files follow you across devices, backups happen automatically, and collaboration is simple.

But here's the part most people miss: The cloud is not inherently secure. The provider protects the infrastructure, but you are responsible for how you use it. If you pick a weak password, share links recklessly, or log in over unprotected Wi-Fi, your cloud account is as vulnerable as leaving a filing cabinet in a public park.

COMMON RISKS: DATA BREACHES, UNSECURED WI-FI, AND SHARED DOCUMENTS

When people hear the term *cloud risk*, they imagine some Hollywood-style mega breach where hackers storm Google or Amazon. Those happen, but more often the weak spot is you.

Data Breaches

Hackers target cloud providers because they're massive treasure troves. When breaches happen, millions of accounts are exposed.

Even if the provider secures their end, weak user credentials often make individual accounts the easiest entry point.

Unsecured Wi-Fi

Coffee shops, airports, hotels—free Wi-Fi feels convenient but often comes with hidden dangers. Attackers set up "evil twin" networks with names like "Starbucks Guest" and capture everything you type, including cloud logins. Without encryption or a VPN, your data is basically broadcast in public.

Careless File Sharing

One of the biggest risks is oversharing. That "anyone with the link" setting sounds harmless until that link gets forwarded or indexed by search engines. Companies have leaked trade secrets, medical records, and even government documents this way.

Device Syncing

Cloud accounts sync across devices. If your phone or laptop is stolen and not properly secured, the thief gets instant access to your files. The cloud multiplies convenience—but also multiplies points of vulnerability.

FILE SHARING: THE DOS AND DON'TS

- Do share with specific people; don't open up the share settings to "anyone with the link." That public link could be forwarded to anyone, anywhere. Unless something is really public (which few things are), do not use public links.

- Don't leave old shared links open forever. Expire them or revoke access once the project ends.
- Do use permissions wisely—view only for most, edit access for only those who need it.
- Don't email sensitive documents as attachments if you can use secure sharing instead. Attachments multiply the number of copies outside your control.
- Do audit your shared files every few months. You'll be surprised how many people still have access to documents they no longer need.

The cloud is powerful. But power without discipline is risk disguised as convenience.

BEST PRACTICES FOR CHOOSING AND USING CLOUD SERVICES

Picking a cloud provider isn't just about price or storage size. It's about trust and security.

Choosing a Cloud Provider

Reputation and Transparency

Stick with major providers (Google Drive, OneDrive, Dropbox, iCloud) or trusted enterprise services. Avoid small, unknown companies with unclear policies.

Security Features

Look for providers that support encryption, strong sharing controls, and two-factor authentication. If those features aren't available, keep looking.

Compliance Standards

If you run a business, make sure the provider complies with regulations like GDPR (discussed in chapter 3) or HIPAA if you handle sensitive information.

Using the Cloud Wisely

Segment Your Data

Don't dump everything into one account. Separate personal and professional data. Consider using one cloud for sensitive files and another for general use.

Limit Device Access

Only connect devices you actively use. Remove old laptops or phones from your account access list.

Regularly Audit Access

Every three months, review who has access to your files and revoke unnecessary permissions.

Set Expiry Dates for Links

Most services allow links to expire. Use this feature. Temporary access is safer than perpetual access.

Back Up Critical Files Separately

The cloud is not infallible. Keep a local backup of critical files in case your account is compromised or the service goes down.

ENCRYPTION, STRONG PASSWORDS, AND TWO-FACTOR AUTHENTICATION

These are the three pillars of cloud security—the habits that separate safe users from victims.

Encryption

Encryption scrambles your data into unreadable code unless you have the right key. Cloud providers encrypt files on their servers, but you can go further:

- Use apps like VeraCrypt or Boxcryptor to encrypt sensitive files before uploading. With VeraCrypt, you create an "encrypted container"—a special file that acts like a secure folder. Anything you drag into it is automatically scrambled with strong encryption, and only someone with the correct password or key can open it. Boxcryptor works a little differently: It integrates with cloud services like Dropbox, OneDrive, or Google Drive. When you save a file into your Boxcryptor folder, it looks normal in your cloud account, but the contents are unreadable gibberish without your encryption key. In both cases, if someone hacks your cloud storage, what they see is just encrypted data—not your private documents.
- If you're handling legal, financial, or health

information, using pre-encryption programs like these gives you control even if the provider is breached.

Strong Passwords

Passwords remain the front door to your cloud account. Weak or reused passwords are like leaving that door unlocked. Here are some best practices:

- Use long passphrases (e.g., "SilverMountain!Train42").
- Never reuse passwords between accounts.
- Use a password manager to keep track of them all.

TWO-FACTOR AUTHENTICATION

Even the best password can be stolen. 2FA adds a second layer: a code sent to your phone, an authenticator app, or a hardware key.

- Always enable 2FA on cloud accounts.
- Prefer authenticator apps (Google Authenticator, Authy) or hardware keys over SMS, which can be hijacked through SIM swaps.

HOW AI SUPERCHARGES ATTACKS ON THE CLOUD

The attack on Jasmine—the freelance photographer from the beginning of this chapter—wasn't just the result of weak passwords and careless Wi-Fi use. It was amplified by a new reality: Attackers are now using artificial intelligence to target the very cloud services we rely on.

For years, cloud breaches relied on brute force—guessing passwords, stealing tokens, or tricking users with generic phishing emails. Those tactics still exist, but AI has made them faster, more sophisticated, and harder to detect.

Here's how AI is changing the game in terms of cloud security:

1. Automated Credential Attacks

Attackers feed massive stolen password databases into AI systems that can quickly identify weak or reused credentials. Instead of blindly guessing, AI learns which password and username combinations are most likely to work for which cloud service sites, shaving hours or days off a traditional brute-force attempt.

2. Smarter Phishing Against Cloud Apps

AI crafts phishing emails that mimic real login pages for Google Drive, Microsoft 365, or Dropbox. These fake sites look pixel perfect and are customized for the target, right down to the company logo, colors, and even the user's recent activity. Employees often don't realize they've handed over cloud credentials until it's too late.

3. AI-Driven Malware in Shared Documents

Cloud platforms make it easy to share files—but AI helps attackers create malicious documents that appear harmless. An AI model can embed malicious code in a way that slips past filters and antivirus scanners, delivering malware through what looks like a routine PDF or spreadsheet.

4. Exploiting Misconfigurations

Cloud environments are complex, and humans make mistakes—like leaving a storage bucket public or a server unpatched. A storage bucket is just a container where cloud providers like Amazon, Google, or Microsoft let you store files. By default, it should be private, but if an administrator misconfigures the settings, the bucket can be exposed to the open internet. That's how sensitive data like medical records, customer information, or company documents sometimes end up searchable by anyone who knows where to look. An unpatched server is another common problem: When software vendors release updates to fix security holes, organizations have to apply those patches. If they don't, attackers can target those known weaknesses to break in. Together, these missteps create open doors—misconfigured storage buckets leak data, while unpatched servers invite intrusions. AI tools now scour the internet 24-7 for these weak spots, often finding them faster than human defenders, which means even small oversights can quickly become large-scale breaches.

5. Business Email Compromised at Scale

AI doesn't just write generic phishing emails anymore. It can mimic the writing style of a CEO, CFO, or manager by analyzing public emails and documents. This allows attackers to trick employees into sharing sensitive files or approving fraudulent access to cloud accounts.

The result? The cloud, once seen as safer than on-premises

storage, is now a primary target for AI-enhanced attacks. Attackers don't need to break into Google or Microsoft directly—they just need to exploit a weak password, a sloppy sharing setting, or an unpatched server. AI makes finding and exploiting those cracks faster and cheaper than ever before.

The takeaway is sobering but empowering: The same technology that makes attackers stronger can also make defenders smarter. To stay safe in the cloud, you must be as intentional about using AI-driven defenses as criminals are about using AI-driven attacks.

HOW AI PROTECTS THE CLOUD— AND HOW YOU CAN USE IT TOO

It's easy to feel discouraged when you hear how attackers use AI to target the cloud. But here's the encouraging side of the story: Cloud providers are also using AI as their strongest line of defense. The same technology that criminals exploit is being harnessed by companies like Google, Microsoft, Amazon, and Dropbox to protect billions of accounts every day.

How Cloud Providers Use AI to Defend Your Data

Anomaly Detection at Scale

AI systems constantly monitor logins across millions of users. If someone tries to log in to your account from Moscow at two in the morning while you normally log in from Chicago at nine, the system flags it instantly. Instead of relying on you to notice, AI acts as a 24-7 sentry.

Malware Scanning and File Integrity

Every document uploaded to Google Drive, OneDrive, or Dropbox is scanned by AI-driven engines. These models look for hidden code, unusual file behavior, or suspicious metadata that human reviewers would never spot.

Adaptive Authentication

Ever been asked to verify your identity when logging in from a new device? That's AI at work. Cloud providers analyze login behavior in real time and challenge suspicious attempts with extra authentication steps.

Predictive Risk Models

AI doesn't just react; it predicts. By analyzing attack trends across millions of accounts, providers can proactively block IP addresses, domains, or file types before they reach you.

HOW YOU CAN USE AI TO PROTECT YOUR CLOUD APPLICATIONS

Enable AI-Driven Security Features

Many providers hide powerful options in their settings. For example, Microsoft 365's Advanced Threat Protection uses AI to filter phishing emails and malicious links. Google Workspace deploys AI-based spam detection. Turn these on—they're included in many accounts but are often overlooked.

Use AI-Powered Identity Protection

Services like Okta, Autho, or even consumer identity platforms use AI to detect suspicious login attempts. Some password managers now integrate AI to scan the dark web for your credentials and alert you if they appear in breaches.

Use AI Fraud Detection in Financial Apps

If your cloud usage includes banking or payment platforms, enable real-time transaction alerts. These systems use AI to analyze spending patterns and will notify you of unusual behavior—like a sudden charge from across the globe.

Use Personal AI Assistants for Security Hygiene

New security apps use AI to coach you—reminding you to update passwords, alerting you about unsafe sharing, or suggesting when to revoke access to old files. Think of it as a digital security coach keeping you honest.

Leverage AI-Powered Backup Solutions

Some backup services now use AI to flag ransomware-like behavior—such as files suddenly being encrypted or renamed—and automatically preserve safe versions of your data.

The bottom line: AI is not only the hacker's secret weapon—it's also built into the strongest defenses you have. AI is your silent bodyguard in the cloud—always watching, always learning, and always adapting to keep your data safe. The key is to turn these features on, pay attention to the alerts, and let AI serve as the bodyguard that never sleeps, watching over your files and accounts even when you aren't.

SIMPLE BUT POWERFUL SOLUTIONS

The cloud has transformed the way we live and work. It's where we store our photos, run our businesses, share our ideas, and manage our finances. But that same convenience comes with a price: Every file you upload, every link you share, and every account you create becomes a potential target. The story of Jasmine isn't an outlier—it's a warning of what can happen when we treat the cloud as if it were automatically safe.

Attackers know this. They exploit weak passwords, careless sharing, and unsecured Wi-Fi. And now, with artificial intelligence, they can find and attack those weaknesses faster than ever before. What used to take hours of effort can now be automated and scaled to millions of accounts with chilling precision.

But the cloud is not a doomed environment. Far from it. The same AI that empowers attackers also stands ready to defend you. Cloud providers are using machine learning to scan for anomalies, block malicious files, and predict threats before they reach you. As a user, you have access to these same protections—if you take the time to turn them on and use them.

The essentials are simple but powerful: Choose reputable providers, use strong and unique passwords, enable two-factor authentication, encrypt sensitive files, and regularly review who has access to your data. Add to that the AI-driven defenses available in most modern platforms, and suddenly the balance shifts. The cloud becomes not just a place of risk but a place of resilience.

The cloud is not inherently safe or unsafe. It reflects your choices. Used carelessly, it can expose your life and work to strangers in seconds. Used wisely, it becomes one of the most secure, flexible, and empowering tools at your disposal.

The question isn't whether the cloud will be part of your future—it already is. The real question is whether you'll use it as a liability . . . or as a fortress.

KEY TAKEAWAYS

- ☐ Cloud convenience comes with shared responsibility. The provider secures the infrastructure—but you must secure your account.
- ☐ The cloud is just someone else's computer. Treat it with the same caution you'd use with your own.
- ☐ File sharing should be intentional—specific people, limited time, limited permissions.
- ☐ Common risks include weak passwords, public Wi-Fi, and careless sharing.
- ☐ Choose reputable providers, review access regularly, and separate personal from professional data.
- ☐ Encrypt sensitive files before uploading, use strong passwords, and enable two-factor authentication.
- ☐ The cloud is powerful and safe—if you use it wisely. With discipline and the right habits, you can enjoy the freedom of the cloud without exposing yourself to unnecessary risk.

FINAL CHECKLIST: CLOUD SECURITY IN FIVE STEPS

Use Strong, Unique Passwords

- ☐ Never reuse passwords. Store them in a password manager.

Enable Two-Factor Authentication

- ☐ Always add an extra layer of protection for logins.

Encrypt Sensitive Files

- ☐ Use built-in or third-party tools to protect critical data before uploading.

Audit Sharing and Access Regularly

- ☐ Review who has access to your files every few months.
- ☐ Revoke what's no longer needed.

Turn On AI-Driven Protections

- ☐ Make sure cloud security alerts, suspicious login detection, and malware scanning are enabled.

Follow these five steps, and you'll transform the cloud from a soft target into a secure foundation for your work and life.

CHAPTER 7

SOCIAL MEDIA AND PUBLIC SHARING

Back in 2010, a provocative website called PleaseRobMe.com appeared on the internet. Its creators weren't criminals—they were concerned technologists trying to raise awareness about the dangers of oversharing online.

The site worked like this: It aggregated public posts from Twitter and other platforms on which people announced they were leaving for vacations. It combined that with publicly available real estate records to show the value of their homes. Then, it presented an interactive map: "Here are houses worth $500,000, $800,000, or more in this zip code, and their owners just announced they'll be gone for the next ten days."

It was chilling. Imagine coming home from a trip to Hawaii and realizing a stranger could have entered your zip code, found your property, and known with certainty that you weren't home—all without breaking a single law. PleaseRobMe.com itself wasn't illegal. It didn't hack anyone's data. It just connected the dots from what people freely shared.

While PleaseRobMe.com was eventually taken down after public backlash, it left behind a sobering truth: Social media can expose you and your family to real-world danger without your even realizing it. Criminals no longer need to follow you around to know when you're gone or where you live—you're telling them yourself, often in real time.

Here's the kicker: Most people still do it. Posting vacation countdowns, sharing birthday details, geotagging photos at home, posting expensive new purchases—each of these digital breadcrumbs can be pieced together by criminals for scams, identity theft, or even physical crimes.

A few quick tips—before we dive deeper into this chapter—illustrate just how simple it is to cut off some of these risks:

- *Keep accounts private*: If you're posting about your family, children, or vacations, your audience should be trusted friends, not millions of strangers.
- *Strip photo metadata*: Smartphones automatically embed location data into images. That cute picture of your dog in the backyard can also broadcast your home address.
- *Think before you post*: Would you be comfortable if a stranger followed you down the street, snapping pictures of your home, car, or kids? Probably not. But through social media, you might be handing out the same information voluntarily.

Oversharing online is like leaving your house with the front door wide open. You might feel safe in the moment, but you're making yourself a target in ways you'll only realize after it's too late.

RECOGNIZING SOCIAL MEDIA SCAMS AND IMPERSONATION ATTEMPTS

One of the fastest-growing threats on social platforms is impersonation. Criminals don't need to hack your account to exploit your reputation—they can simply mimic it.

Take the story of my friend, whose Facebook account was compromised. His contacts suddenly received frantic messages: "Hey, I'm stuck in Mexico. I was robbed. Can you send $500 so I can get home?" The request sounded urgent and emotional, with all the hallmarks of a scam. Luckily, his friends knew him well enough to realize something was off. No one sent money.

But not everyone is so fortunate. Scammers know that trust is social currency. Once they slip into your digital identity—whether by hacking your account or creating a lookalike—they leverage your relationships. And it works.

Common social media scams include the following:

- *Romance scams*: Criminals build fake profiles, build emotional connections, and then start asking for money.
- *Prize or giveaway scams*: "You won a free iPhone—just click this link."
- *Investment scams*: Fraudsters impersonate influencers or friends, pitching "sure-fire" cryptocurrency or stock tips.
- *Account recovery scams*: Hackers message you claiming to be support staff, asking for your login or recovery codes.

Here are some red flags to identify impersonation scams:

- Messages with urgency and emotional pressure
- Requests for money or gift cards
- Unusual tone or language inconsistent with the person's normal communication
- Duplicate accounts of people you already follow

When in doubt, verify. If you get a suspicious message, call or text the person directly. Never trust an urgent request made solely through social media.

HOW AI IS TRANSFORMING SOCIAL MEDIA THREATS

The PleaseRobMe.com story showed how easy it is to misuse public information that people share online. That was more than a decade ago—before artificial intelligence was in the hands of criminals. Today, the risks have multiplied because AI gives attackers new ways to exploit every photo, post, and update we share.

In the past, scammers had to manually write messages, copy and paste posts, and hope they could trick a few people. Now, AI can generate thousands of tailored scams in seconds—each one polished, convincing, and personalized to the target.

AI presents similar challenges to social media that I've introduced previously—such as hyperrealistic impersonation scraped from your past posts or deepfakes mimicking your voice—but there are new dangers from AI specifically related to public sharing:

1. Automated Oversharing Exploitation

AI tools scrape massive numbers of public posts to build detailed profiles of individuals: where you live, where you vacation, who your family members are, where you work. Instead of criminals piecing this together manually, AI organizes it instantly, making targeted scams more efficient than ever.

2. *Social Engineering at Scale*

Attackers once needed to choose a handful of victims. With AI, they can target millions, tailoring scams based on each person's public information. One person might get a fake job offer, another a fake charity request, another a phishing link—all crafted to match their life.

3. *Disinformation and Manipulation*

AI-generated content floods platforms with fake news, polarizing opinions, and fabricated "evidence." This doesn't just threaten individuals—it erodes trust across society, making it harder to separate truth from lies.

The result is sobering: Social media threats are no longer clumsy or easy to spot. They are precise, scalable, and increasingly indistinguishable from genuine communication. AI has turned oversharing from a personal risk into a mass vulnerability. AI has made social media scams smarter, faster, and harder to spot. What you share publicly is now more valuable—and more dangerous—than ever.

The good news? Awareness and stronger security habits can still protect you. But the margin for error is smaller than ever before.

THE DANGERS OF OVERSHARING

We tend to think of danger online in terms of dramatic hacks. But the truth is, attackers often don't need advanced tools. They need only your own posts.

Oversharing is a gold mine for criminals because small details add up:

- *Location check-ins*: Announcing that you're at the airport for a weeklong trip signals an empty home.
- *Birthday posts*: Sharing your child's exact birth date gives identity thieves answers to common security questions.
- *Job updates*: Announcing a promotion can make you a target for spear phishing, where attackers pose as vendors or executives.
- *Photos at home*: Background details like mail on the counter, street numbers, or Wi-Fi names can reveal more than you think.
- *New automobile*: Announcing a new acquisition like this allows attackers to target you, your lifestyle, your net worth, and possibly where you and your family live.

Here's how attackers use oversharing:

- *Credential cracking*: Using your pet's name, birthday, or child's name—often visible in posts—as part of password guessing
- *Spear phishing*: Crafting convincing messages tailored to your life, like fake vacation rental receipts after you post about travel
- *Perpetrating physical crime*: Knowing when you're out of town or what valuables you own
- *Attacking reputation*: Taking your words or photos out of context and using them against you

Social media is not a diary. It's a megaphone. Every detail you post, no matter how small, becomes part of the public record criminals can exploit.

DEEPFAKES AND THE BLURRING OF REALITY

In the past, spotting a fake profile or scam was easier. The grammar was bad, the photos were stock images, and the lies were clumsy. Not anymore.

Enter deepfakes—AI-generated videos and audio that look and sound real. Criminals can now create a convincing video of someone saying or doing something they never did. Or they can generate a phone call in a loved one's voice, asking for money.

The danger is not just embarrassment—it's trust erosion. If you can't believe your own eyes or ears, how do you know what's real? Deepfakes are already being used for things like these:

- *Financial scams*: Fraudsters clone a CEO's voice to authorize fake wire transfers.
- *Revenge attacks*: Criminals generate compromising videos of individuals to extort them.
- *Political misinformation*: Fake speeches and interviews designed to sway opinion.

The lesson: Skepticism must become a habit. If a video, photo, or voice recording seems too shocking—or perfectly timed—it might not be real. Always verify information through multiple trusted sources.

SECURING YOUR SOCIAL MEDIA ACCOUNTS

The threats are serious, but so are the defenses. Securing your accounts isn't complicated—it just requires discipline.

Privacy Settings

- Make accounts private when sharing personal details.
- Limit who can see your posts, tag you, or send friend requests.
- Regularly review your friend/follower list, and remove people you don't actually know.

Strong Passwords

- Use long, unique passphrases for each account.
- Never reuse passwords across platforms.
- Store them in a password manager.

Multi-Factor Authentication

- Enable MFA on every account.
- Prefer authenticator apps or hardware keys over SMS.
- Some platforms (like Facebook and Instagram) allow you to review active sessions—log out of unfamiliar devices.

Account Recovery

- Update recovery emails and phone numbers.
- Remove outdated contact info that could be exploited.
- Add trusted contacts if the platform offers the option.

Regular Audits

- Review app permissions—many third-party apps connected to your account no longer need access.
- Check login history for suspicious activity.
- Search for duplicate accounts impersonating you.

HOW SOCIAL MEDIA PROVIDERS USE AI TO PROTECT YOU

The same artificial intelligence that attackers use to exploit social media is also being deployed by the platforms themselves to defend you. Companies like Meta (Facebook, Instagram), X (formerly Twitter), LinkedIn, and TikTok run billions of accounts, and manual monitoring is impossible. AI has become their primary weapon to keep users safe.

Here's how they're using it:

1. Detecting Fake Accounts

AI models analyze new accounts the moment they're created. If the behavior matches known patterns of bots or impersonators—such as posting at abnormal speeds, recycling stolen profile pictures, or sending hundreds of friend requests in minutes—the system automatically flags or removes them before they reach you.

2. Phishing and Scam Detection

Platforms scan billions of messages daily using AI to detect suspicious links, urgent language, or patterns consistent with scams. These messages can be quarantined, hidden, or flagged with warnings so you know before you click.

3. Deepfake and Content Recognition

AI image and video recognition tools now scan uploaded content for signs of manipulation. This helps detect deepfake pornography, fraudulent videos, or stolen images used in scams. While not perfect, these systems are improving rapidly and prevent millions of harmful posts from spreading.

4. Login and Behavior Monitoring

Social networks track your normal login habits—like the devices, locations, and times you typically access your account. If someone tries to log in from another country or in a way that looks unusual, AI can trigger identity checks such as email or two-factor verification.

5. Hate Speech, Fraud, and Misinformation Filtering

Beyond direct scams, AI moderates harmful content at scale—catching misinformation campaigns, spammy promotions, or coordinated fraud rings that would otherwise flood your feed.

6. Account Recovery and Alerts

If your account is compromised, AI-driven systems can help you recover it. For example, Facebook uses AI to recognize whether a compromised account is behaving abnormally and then lock it until you verify your identity.

Social media platforms are under constant attack, and they know their survival depends on user trust. That's why they're investing heavily in AI defense systems—watching, filtering, and analyzing at a scale no human team ever could. But these protections only help if you turn on account alerts, enable two-factor authentication, and pay attention to the warnings they provide.

> But remember, this security is a two-way street. While social media providers are using AI to protect you, they are also using AI to perform targeted marketing on your interests to drive revenue from paid ads. Therefore, you should always limit the information you post and turn on privacy settings.

HOW YOU CAN USE AI TO PROTECT YOURSELF ON SOCIAL MEDIA

Social media platforms deploy AI behind the scenes, but you can also bring AI into your own corner of the fight. Today, many of the best security tools available to consumers are powered by AI, and when combined with smart habits, they give you the upper hand.

AI-Powered Password Managers

Password managers like 1Password, Dashlane, or LastPass now use AI to analyze your credentials. They'll flag weak, reused, or breached passwords and suggest stronger replacements. This prevents attackers from exploiting the same simple passwords across multiple accounts.

Scam and Spam Filters

AI-based browser extensions and third-party apps can filter direct messages, comments, and links for scam patterns. Instead of manually spotting suspicious language, AI does it for you—warning you before you click.

AI Identity Monitoring

Services like Aura, IdentityForce, and others scan the dark web using AI to detect if your email, phone number, or social media credentials have been leaked. You'll get an alert immediately if your information shows up for sale, giving you time to change passwords before attackers strike.

Smarter Privacy Coaches

Some security tools now act like digital assistants, analyzing your social media profiles for overexposure. They'll warn you if your settings are too open, if your posts are revealing sensitive data (like addresses in photos), or if your personal details are easy to scrape.

Fraud Detection in Linked Accounts

AI-driven alerts in banking and e-commerce apps connected to your social profiles can notify you of suspicious logins, fake account linkages, or fraudulent activity triggered by compromised social credentials.

Content Verification Tools

AI-powered tools like Deepware Scanner and others help you verify whether an image or video you receive is a deepfake. This is especially valuable in spotting disinformation or impersonation attempts that target your trust.

Attackers are using AI to make scams harder to detect, but you don't have to fight blindly. By enabling AI-based tools—password managers, dark web monitoring, scam filters, and deepfake detectors—you put another layer of defense between yourself and the criminals. Think of it as having an AI bodyguard standing between you and the endless stream of scams flooding social media.

TOP FIVE AI TOOLS TO USE ON SOCIAL MEDIA TODAY

AI-Powered Password Manager

Use tools like 1Password or Dashlane to create strong, unique passwords and get alerts if they've been exposed.

AI Scam and Spam Filters

Enable platform filters and consider third-party tools that scan messages and comments for suspicious language or links.

AI Identity Monitoring

Use services like Aura or IdentityForce to monitor the dark web for your leaked social media credentials.

AI Privacy Coach

Leverage tools that review your posts and profile settings, warning you if you're oversharing sensitive data.

AI Deepfake and Content Verification

Use AI detection apps like Deepware Scanner to spot manipulated videos or photos before you trust or share them.

AI is not just the attacker's tool—it's your shield. By enabling these protections, you make your social media accounts harder to compromise and easier to defend.

YOU CREATE YOUR OWN RISK

Social media is woven into the fabric of modern life. It connects us with friends, helps us celebrate milestones, and even builds careers. But it also exposes us in ways no generation has faced before. Every status update, every photo, every shared detail can become a thread in a web spun by attackers.

From awareness-raising projects like PleaseRobMe.com to

the rise of deepfakes and impersonation scams, the risks are evolving as fast as the platforms themselves. The difference between being a victim and staying safe often comes down to choices: whether you keep your accounts private, whether you use strong authentication, whether you pause before posting personal details.

The truth is simple but powerful: Social media itself isn't dangerous. How you use it determines the risk. Shared carelessly, it can put your reputation, finances, and even physical safety in jeopardy. Used wisely, it can remain a positive, empowering part of your life.

The next time you're about to post, ask yourself this: "Am I sharing this with friends—or with the entire world?" That small shift in perspective can be the line between safety and exposure.

KEY TAKEAWAYS

- ☐ Social media is a powerful tool—but it's also a hunting ground for criminals. Oversharing and weak account security make you the prey.
- ☐ Sites like PleaseRobMe.com showed how easily public posts can be exploited for real-world crime.
- ☐ Impersonation scams prey on trust, often asking friends and family for money.
- ☐ Oversharing details like birthdays, travel, or job changes gives criminals ammunition.
- ☐ Deepfakes are blurring the line between truth and lies—verify before you trust.
- ☐ Protect yourself with privacy settings, strong passwords, MFA, and regular audits.
- ☐ Every post is permanent, every detail is valuable, and every account is a potential target. Social media doesn't have to be dangerous—but only if you use it with awareness and discipline.

FINAL CHECKLIST: SOCIAL MEDIA SAFETY IN FIVE STEPS

- ☐ *Lock Down Privacy Settings:* Make your accounts private if you share personal details. Limit who can see, tag, or message you.
- ☐ *Use Strong, Unique Passwords:* Every account gets its own passphrase. Store them in a password manager—never reuse.
- ☐ *Turn On Multi-Factor Authentication:* Always enable MFA (preferably with an authenticator app or security key) to stop account takeovers.
- ☐ *Think Before You Post:* Avoid announcing travel plans, oversharing birthdays, or posting photos that reveal locations or valuables.
- ☐ *Audit Your Accounts Regularly:* Review followers, third-party app connections, and recent logins. Revoke access and log out of unknown sessions.

Bottom line: Social media can connect and empower you—but only if you stay in control of what you share, how you secure it, and whom you allow into your digital circle.

CHAPTER 8

STREAMING YOUR LIFE AWAY

Mark considered himself tech savvy. He worked in finance, had the latest iPhone, and prided himself on knowing "how not to get scammed." However, as I've mentioned before, common sense is not common practice. Common sense in the real world does not spill over into digital.

It was a rainy Saturday night when the hack began. Scrolling through social media, Mark saw a post: "Watch the latest block-buster for free—HD quality, no ads."

The link looked harmless. The page had the movie poster, Rotten Tomatoes score, and a "Play Now" button. When Mark clicked it, the site told him he needed to "install a video codec" to watch. He hesitated for a moment—even googled around to see if this was a scam or not, and it seemed like this kind of offering was relatively common. The promise of free, instant access won him out. The download took seconds. The movie started playing . . . but after a minute, it froze. Mark shrugged, closed the page, and went back to Netflix.

What Mark didn't know was that the "codec" was actually a remote access trojan (referred to as RAT in the hacker community). While he watched Netflix, a hacker in Eastern Europe had already gained silent access to his laptop. They scanned his hard drive, captured his saved passwords, and even activated his webcam briefly—just to prove they could. This is what we call a drive-by download. Essentially, the attacker waits for you to click a link or accept a download, and your life is stolen.

In the moment, Mark was tired and figured the freezing was merely a glitch. He kept his computer connected to the internet and got some sleep. By Monday morning, he began to recognize the extent of the damage:

- His PayPal account had unauthorized transfers.
- His email inbox was flooded with password reset requests.
- Files from his work laptop (which he occasionally used at home) were stolen—client lists, contracts, and sensitive financial data.

When IT at his company detected suspicious logins from overseas, they called Mark immediately. They had to shut down his accounts, freeze his corporate access, and begin a costly forensic investigation. Mark later learned that the same "free streaming" link had been part of a coordinated malware campaign targeting thousands of people. The attackers monetized stolen accounts on the dark web, sold his data to identity thieves, and ransomed some of his personal files back to him for Bitcoin.

The total cost—between identity recovery services, lost work hours, and personal losses—was over $15,000. All for a movie ticket he could have bought for twelve dollars.

Mark learned a big lesson that day: Attackers know that curiosity, boredom, and the lure of "free" are more powerful than technical safeguards. One careless click on a streaming site can open the door to full digital compromise. Attackers have no morals or ethics, so they go after good people, ethical people, and moral people without reservations.

Sometimes when I travel, I have to walk through bad parts of a city in order to get in my morning workout. Usually, I am up at four thirty in the morning and am in the gym by five, where I get my mental clarity. And while I always try to plan out the safest route, sometimes I have to go through some rough areas. When I do, I take different security precautions. I take off my headphones, pay attention, and stay alert. I operate differently than if I am in a safe park on a sunny day.

In the same way I keep my headphones out and pay attention as I walk through a bad neighborhood, you should not click on links and not download anything. It is better to avoid watching a movie than having your life ruined.

TOP ATTACKS ON STREAMING SITES

Streaming video has transformed entertainment, education, and communication. Platforms like Netflix, YouTube, Hulu, Amazon Prime Video, Twitch, and Disney+ have become as integral to daily life as email. Families gather for Netflix nights, kids watch cartoons on YouTube, sports fans tune in to live matches, and grandparents video call relatives on smart TVs. But with the convenience of on-demand access comes a new set of cybersecurity concerns—many of which the average user never considers.

People often ask, "How can we stay ahead of the attackers? How do we know what the attackers are going to target?" The answer is simple: Follow the money, and follow the market growth. Where money and people exist, there will be attackers. As markets grow and expand, so do the attackers. Monetary-driven attacks such as credit cards, access to accounts, credentials, and identities are all prime targets. Services like video streamers have all these qualities and therefore have created a fertile breeding ground for attackers.

The global video streaming market was valued last year at $674 billion and projected to grow to $811 billion over the next five years to reach a growth of just under $3 trillion. That factors out to a compound annual growth rate of 18.5 percent. Attackers know all this and will continue to target streaming, and anyone who engages in it (which nowadays is pretty much everyone).

There are ten main cybersecurity concerns with streaming video:

Account Takeover and Credential Theft

This is when a hacker will gain your account credentials to sell them to other people. These credentials are then sold on the dark web so that people can get low-cost access to streaming video services or are used to test stolen credentials for other platforms.

For example, in late 2022, thousands of Disney+ accounts were found for sale within days of the service's launch. Most had been compromised through password reuse. There is nothing Disney+ could have done about this. This was not caused because of a breach or compromise of Disney+ servers; it was because users, just like you and me, used the same password across multiple accounts. This is why one of the themes of this book is that you can have the safest car, but without a safe driver, accidents can still happen. The Disney+ password issues show that even when servers were secure (a safe car was provided), users were at risk because of poor practices of password reuse (unsafe driver).

> **Risks:** Loss of personal access, potential exposure of stored payment information, and cross-platform compromise if the same password is used elsewhere

Data Privacy and Behavioral Tracking

Streaming services gather massive amounts of user data, including watch history, device identifiers, geolocation, and interaction patterns. There is a song from the 1980s whose lyrics say, "Every move you make, every breath you take, I am watching you." This is exactly what happens when you are using anything digital or any service such as streaming. Everything you do is being watched, recorded, and monitored. Some people say, "Who cares if someone knows I am watching a certain movie?" But that's not all that streaming services know about you. More and more authentication and verification are based on user behavior, so accessing your streaming information can make it easier for someone to impersonate you and/or target you or your family.

All this happens through back-end systems that are designed to track and monitor your behavior. This data is collected through app analytics, content recommendation systems, and third-party ad trackers embedded within the platform. Over time, these platforms can build highly detailed behavioral profiles that could be exposed in a breach, sold to advertisers, or subpoenaed in legal cases.

When you sign up for a streaming service, there is always a ULA (user license agreement) that you are required to acknowledge or digitally sign without even realizing it. The agreements are often long, and very few people actually read them. Therefore, it is important to review your streaming app's privacy settings, limit permissions (such as location tracking), and consider using a VPN to obscure your IP address.

Fo example, in 2023, privacy advocates raised concerns when it was revealed that multiple streaming apps were sending viewing data to advertising networks without clear user consent. In addition to writing books and sharing my knowledge with the world to secure cyberspace, I also perform expert witness work in trials. One area in which we are seeing a huge rise in cases filed is the area of data privacy and situations where the provider of a service was tracking data and information without the user knowing it, but it was often in excess of what was reasonable under the circumstances.

> **Risks:** In the short term, not much can be done to stop the streaming sites from collecting so much information on you, and you just have to be aware and careful of what you do with streaming services. Streaming services are increasingly allowing opt-out options for the user to limit the tracking, but you have to go in and do the work of selecting these options.

Malware from Fake Streaming Sites

The lure of "free" streaming is a common trap. Criminals create look-alike websites offering pirated or early-release content, often requiring the user to download a fake "video player" or codec. The download is actually malware—anything from adware to full-blown ransomware. In 2020, a global malware campaign used fake movie sites to spread the Azorult trojan, which stole browser passwords and cryptocurrency wallets.

> **Risks:** Complete compromise of the victim's device, theft of sensitive files, and unauthorized access to accounts

Man-in-the-Middle (MITM) Attacks

Streaming on unsecured public Wi-Fi can expose your data to interception. If the platform's connection isn't fully encrypted, attackers on the same network can hijack your session or steal login credentials. Security researchers have demonstrated that poorly configured streaming apps can leak authentication tokens, giving attackers account access without needing a password.

> **Risks:** Stolen account sessions, personal data theft, and even exposure of stored payment methods

Piracy and Illegal Content Risks

Accessing pirated streams isn't just a legal risk—it's a security risk. Unofficial streaming services and torrent-based platforms are breeding grounds for malware, often hiding malicious code inside video files or player applications. For example, several piracy apps distributed through third-party Android stores were discovered to contain banking trojans disguised as video players. In one campaign, security researchers uncovered more than twenty malicious apps that had been downloaded hundreds of thousands of times across Southeast Asia and Eastern Europe. These apps not only stole banking credentials but also granted attackers remote control of the device, allowing them to intercept text messages and bypass two-factor authentication. The scale was large enough that banks in multiple countries had to issue emergency advisories to customers, and some app stores were forced to shut down sections of their catalog.

Risks: Infection with spyware or ransomware and, in some jurisdictions, prosecution for consuming or distributing copyrighted content

Digital Rights Management and Content Protection Exploits

Digital rights management (DRM) systems protect streaming content from unauthorized copying, but they can be exploited. DRM systems are designed to protect copyrighted content such as movies, TV shows, and music by controlling how digital media is accessed, shared, and stored. When you stream a show on Netflix or listen to a track on Spotify, DRM ensures that the content is decrypted only within approved apps or devices. From the user's perspective, this makes it seamless: You can enjoy content instantly without needing to download or manage files, while creators and distributors gain confidence that their work isn't being freely copied or pirated.

However, DRM also comes with trade-offs. Because it enforces restrictions on how digital media can be used, users may find they cannot watch content offline without special permissions, transfer files between devices, or make backups—even for personal use. This sometimes frustrates consumers, who feel they paid for the content but don't fully control it. Meanwhile, pirates often look for ways to break DRM, meaning that while legitimate users are restricted, determined attackers may still find ways around the protections.

What makes DRM particularly important in cybersecurity discussions is that it represents a double-edged sword: While it safeguards intellectual property, the complexity of these systems can create new vulnerabilities. Attackers who reverse engineer DRM modules may discover flaws they can exploit, not only to bypass restrictions but also to plant malware or steal user data. Attackers can reverse engineer playback software to extract decryption keys or capture raw video streams. In this way, DRM highlights the tension between usability, security, and control—reminding us that protective measures, if misapplied or poorly secured, can themselves become attack surfaces.

In 2021, a vulnerability in a popular browser's Widevine DRM implementation allowed pirates to bypass protections and redistribute premium video content. Widevine is Google's DRM technology, built into Chrome and widely adopted by Netflix, Disney+, Amazon Prime, and other streaming platforms, which meant the flaw had global reach. Security researchers demonstrated that with only moderate technical skill, attackers could intercept the decrypted video stream before it was re-encrypted, essentially stripping away all the protections. This made it possible to copy movies in full HD quality and redistribute them through piracy networks within hours of their release. The scale was significant because Widevine is not a niche system—it is the backbone DRM solution for billions of devices worldwide, from laptops and smartphones to smart TVs.

The incident underscored how a single weakness in a common DRM platform can cascade across the entire entertainment ecosystem. Instead of one app or service being compromised, every streaming provider that relied on Widevine was theoretically at risk. Studios and distributors feared massive revenue losses as leaked titles spread quickly across torrent sites and illicit streaming services. While the vulnerability was eventually patched, the episode highlighted that DRM is both a critical safeguard and a potential single point of failure. It also illustrated the broader tension in cybersecurity: The very systems meant to enforce trust can themselves become weak links that attackers exploit at scale.

> **Risks:** Stolen intellectual property, platform reputation damage, and legal disputes

Internet of Things and Smart TV Vulnerabilities

Streaming doesn't just happen on laptops and phones—smart TVs, streaming sticks, and game consoles are part of the attack surface. Many of these devices run outdated firmware or use insecure APIs. Some have microphones and cameras that can be exploited. In 2019, for example, hackers demonstrated how certain smart TVs could be remotely accessed to change settings, play fake content, or spy via connected microphones.

> **Risks:** Unauthorized control of your TV, invasion of privacy, and potential access to other devices on your home network

Payment and Subscription Fraud

Cybercriminals exploit weak billing protections to steal money or services. Stolen credit card numbers are used to open new streaming accounts or upgrade existing ones. Others abuse charge-back systems to consume content and then dispute the payment.

For example, criminals will often buy batches of stolen cards on underground forums for just a few dollars each and then test them by setting up Netflix, Hulu, or Disney+ accounts. If the card works, they either resell the "ready-to-watch" accounts cheaply on dark web marketplaces or use them personally until the fraud is detected. For legitimate cardholders, this can mean unexpected charges, frozen accounts, or even finding that their card was used to subscribe to services they've never heard of.

Others abuse charge-back systems to consume content and then dispute the payment, a practice sometimes called "friendly fraud." A user might binge-watch a full season of a show and then claim they never authorized the transaction, triggering a reversal of the charge. While it seems like a victimless loophole, it has real consequences: Platforms lose revenue, payment processors absorb losses, and subscription prices can rise to offset fraud. For consumers, repeated abuse of charge-backs can result in accounts being terminated or banned, sometimes even when disputes were legitimate.

In short, these schemes illustrate that financial fraud in streaming services isn't just about lost dollars—it directly affects user trust, payment security, and the overall sustainability of the content ecosystem. The convenience of one-click sign-ups and instant access, while appealing, is exactly what makes streaming platforms attractive targets for cybercriminals.

Risks: Financial loss, subscription disruptions, and account closure

Manipulation of Recommendation Algorithms

Streaming platforms rely heavily on recommendation engines, which can be gamed by attackers. By flooding platforms with manipulated content or metadata, malicious actors can push disinformation, scams, or extremist propaganda into trending lists.

For example, a coordinated bot network might upload thousands of low-quality clips or fake accounts that all "like" and comment on a particular video. This tricks the algorithm into thinking the content is popular, placing it on trending or recommended feeds where millions of users are more likely to see it. To the average user, it looks organic—just another hot topic everyone is talking about—when in reality it was artificially boosted.

The impact is more than an annoyance. Users may unknowingly engage with manipulated content, whether it's clicking on a scam link, sharing a misleading narrative, or being exposed to extremist material. Because people tend to trust what appears in trending sections, the psychological effect is powerful: False ideas gain credibility simply by appearing popular. For streaming and social platforms, this creates a trust crisis—what users believe to be genuine community interest can actually be a manufactured campaign designed to exploit them.

> **Risks:** Exposure to harmful or false content, targeted radicalization, or phishing scams delivered through platform messaging systems

Weak Encryption and Protocol Flaws

If the underlying streaming technology isn't properly secured, streams and data can be intercepted. Using outdated protocols or misconfigured servers can expose stream keys and personal data. Security researchers have found streaming services leaking API keys in public code repositories, allowing attackers to pull subscriber data.

Security researchers have found streaming services leaking

API keys in public code repositories, allowing attackers to pull subscriber data. In one notable case, researchers discovered that developers had accidentally committed secret keys for a major streaming platform into a public GitHub repository. With those exposed credentials, anyone could query back-end systems as if they were an authorized service, pulling information such as usernames, email addresses, subscription tiers, and even partial payment details. The scope was not theoretical—tests confirmed that attackers could have accessed data on hundreds of thousands of subscribers without triggering alarms.

For users, this means that simply signing up for a streaming account could expose their personal information if the company's developers are not careful with secure coding practices. Once subscriber data is stolen, it often gets resold in underground forums, where it can be combined with other leaks to fuel identity theft, phishing, or account takeover campaigns. What makes these exposures particularly troubling is that they bypass the traditional defenses consumers expect—passwords, two-factor authentication, or encryption don't matter if attackers can pull data directly from the source with a valid key.

Risks: Theft of live stream content, unauthorized restreaming, and data breaches

PROTECTING AND SECURING STREAMING SERVICES

By following a few proven safety measures, you can enjoy your favorite shows and movies while keeping your personal data—and your family—safe.

Lock Down Your Streaming Accounts

Your streaming accounts aren't just for watching TV—they're tied to personal information, payment details, and viewing history.

Tips:

- Use strong, unique passwords for each streaming service. Avoid reusing passwords from other accounts.
- Enable MFA wherever it's available. While not all streaming platforms offer MFA, those that do (like Amazon Prime Video) should have it turned on.
- Review active devices in your account settings, and log out of any you don't recognize.

Family tip:

- If kids have their own streaming profiles, keep them under your main account so you can monitor login activity.

Stream Only from Legitimate Sources

Use of pirated or unofficial streaming sites is one of the most common ways families are exposed to malware, scams, and inappropriate content.

Tips:

- Stick to official apps downloaded from trusted app stores (Google Play, Apple App Store, or your device's official app marketplace).
- Avoid downloading "free movie" apps from unknown websites.
- Be wary of search results or social media links promising early releases of new shows—these are often traps.

Family tip:

- Set parental controls on app stores to prevent kids from downloading unauthorized apps.

Protect Your Home Network

A compromised network is a direct pipeline for hackers into your streaming devices, laptops, and even smart appliances.

Tips:

- Change the default password on your home router to something unique and strong.
- Enable WPA3 encryption if your router supports it, or WPA2 as a minimum.
- Regularly update your router's firmware.
- Consider segmenting your network—putting smart TVs and streaming devices on a separate Wi-Fi network from your work computers and phones.

Family tip:

- Create a separate "guest network" for visiting friends and kids' devices to reduce your exposure.

Use a VPN for Public or Shared Wi-Fi

Streaming at coffee shops, airports, or hotels can leave your family's data exposed to "man-in-the-middle" attacks.

Tips:

- Use a reputable VPN service to encrypt traffic when streaming outside the home.
- Avoid logging in to your streaming accounts on public computers or shared devices.

Family tip:

- Teach older kids and teens about the dangers of logging in to personal accounts on school or public library computers.

Enable Parental Controls and Content Filters

Parental controls aren't just for managing age-appropriate viewing—they're also a layer of security and privacy protection.

Tips:

- Most platforms (Netflix, Disney+, Hulu, YouTube) allow you to restrict viewing by age rating.
- Turn off autoplay to prevent children from unintentionally being exposed to harmful or inappropriate videos.
- Disable chat features on platforms like Twitch to prevent kids from interacting with strangers.

Family tip:

- Review watch history weekly to ensure viewing patterns match your household rules.

Keep Devices and Apps Updated

Outdated software is a hacker's best friend. Vulnerabilities in streaming apps or device firmware can be exploited for data theft or malware installation.

Tips:

- Enable automatic updates on all streaming devices, including smart TVs and set-top boxes.
- Manually check for updates every month if automatic updates aren't available.
- Delete unused apps to reduce the number of potential entry points for attackers.

Family tip:

- Add a monthly "tech check" to your family calendar to update all devices together.

Monitor Data Sharing and Privacy Settings

Streaming services often track viewing habits for recommendations and ads. This data can be excessive—and sometimes sold to third parties.

Tips:

- Review and adjust privacy settings in each streaming account.
- Disable targeted ads where possible.
- Avoid linking your streaming accounts to social media unless necessary.

Family tip:

- Show your kids how their viewing habits can be tracked and why protecting personal information matters.

Watch Out for Phishing Scams

Fake emails or text messages pretending to be from Netflix, Hulu, or Disney+ are a popular method for stealing passwords and payment details.

Tips:

- Verify any message claiming your account is "locked" or "needs payment" by logging in directly through the official app or website—not by clicking links.
- Look for spelling errors, generic greetings ("Dear Customer"), or suspicious sender addresses.
- Enable email spam filters.

Family tip:

- Share real-life phishing examples with older kids so they know what to avoid.

Secure Smart TVs and Streaming Devices

Smart TVs and streaming sticks (Roku, Fire TV, Apple TV, Chromecast) can be hacked if they run outdated firmware or have open network services.

Tips:

- Update device software regularly.
- Disable microphone and camera features unless you specifically need them.
- Turn off features like screen mirroring if not in use.

Family tip:

- Unplug smart TVs or streaming devices overnight if you're concerned about privacy.

Educate the Whole Family

Technology alone won't keep your family safe—habits and awareness are equally important.

Tips:

- Have a family meeting to set basic streaming safety rules.
- Encourage kids to speak up if they see something suspicious or get a strange message on a streaming platform.
- Stay updated on the latest streaming scams and security advisories.

Family tip:

- Make it fun—quiz your kids on spotting scams or challenge them to find the privacy settings in their favorite app.

STREAM SMARTER

Streaming video is here to stay—and so are the cybersecurity threats that come with it. As streaming services continue to grow, the cyberattacks will also continue to occur. The same features that make streaming so convenient—on-demand access, multidevice availability, personalized recommendations—also create openings for cybercriminals.

On-demand access means content is constantly being pulled from cloud servers, which often rely on exposed APIs or poorly secured endpoints. Attackers target these interfaces to scrape content, steal user data, or inject malicious code into the data flow. Multidevice availability, while great for flexibility, multiplies the attack surface: Every smart TV, game console, tablet, and phone connected to a single account is a potential weak link. Compromising one device—such as an outdated TV with no security updates—can give intruders a foothold into the broader account.

Personalized recommendations also rely on massive amounts of data collection, including viewing history, device IDs, and in some cases even location data. If this data is stolen, it can be used for profiling, targeted phishing, or even extortion based on sensitive viewing habits. Worse, recommendation systems can be manipulated by attackers flooding them with fake reviews or automated viewing to push malicious or fraudulent content higher in the feed, increasing the chance that unsuspecting users will click.

For everyday users, these threats translate into risks like stolen payment details, compromised personal information, hijacked accounts sold on the dark web, or exposure to scams disguised as recommended content. In other words, the same frictionless experience that makes streaming feel effortless is exactly what attackers exploit, leveraging the convenience as cover for their attacks.

The trick is not to be scared or to run away from these services but to embrace them and accept that there are practical tips you can take to protect yourself.

For everyday users, security boils down to a few key principles:

- Only use legitimate platforms.
- Keep devices and apps updated.
- Use strong, unique passwords with MFA.
- Avoid public Wi-Fi without a VPN.

For businesses and content providers, the stakes are even higher—customer trust, intellectual property, and revenue all depend on robust security. Streaming may be the future of media, but without the right safeguards, it can also be the gateway to a digital nightmare.

Streaming video should be enjoyable, not a security gamble. By combining good digital hygiene with a few simple technical safeguards, you can protect your accounts, devices, and—most importantly—your family. Cybercriminals know streaming is a daily habit for billions of people, which is why it's a prime target. A little awareness now can prevent a lot of headaches later—so take the time to secure your streaming world today.

KEY TAKEAWAYS

- ☐ Streaming is big business, which means hackers are drawn to it.
- ☐ Streaming sites are subject to the same attacks as other sites and digital infrastructure described earlier, but streaming's massive adoption makes more people vulnerable.
- ☐ The Wi-Fi-connected devices in our home—including smart TVs—open us up to attacks.
- ☐ There are a few simple things you can do to protect yourself from streaming attacks:
- ☐ Only use legitimate platforms.
- ☐ Keep devices and apps updated.
- ☐ Use strong, unique passwords with MFA.
- ☐ Avoid public Wi-Fi without a VPN.

CHAPTER 9:

CYBERSECURITY 101—PRACTICAL HABITS FOR EVERYDAY SAFETY

When most people think about cybersecurity, they imagine complicated tools, expensive software, or a team of IT professionals in a high-tech war room. The truth is far simpler—and much more empowering. The strongest cybersecurity doesn't come from fancy tools. It comes from habits.

Think about physical security for a moment. Locking your front door, setting an alarm, not leaving valuables in your car—these aren't complicated or technical. They're just regular, everyday habits. Do them consistently, and you avoid most crimes of opportunity. Fail to do them, and you make yourself a target.

The same is true online. Hackers don't spend their days writing Hollywood-style code to break into people's lives. Most of the time, they look for low-hanging fruit: weak passwords, out-of-date software, careless clicks, and public oversharing. If you eliminate those easy wins, most criminals will move on to the next target.

This chapter is about giving you a clear, practical, step-by-step playbook you can follow every day to stay safe. No jargon. No complex tools. Just habits you can implement right now that make you dramatically harder to hack.

HABIT #1: NEVER CLICK ON A LINK

If I could give you only one cybersecurity rule to follow for the rest of your life, it would be this: Never click on a link you didn't ask for.

That may sound extreme, even paranoid. After all, the internet is built on links. They connect us from one place to another, from an email to a website, from a text to a payment page. But here's the uncomfortable truth: Links are also the number one weapon attackers use to trick people. They are the entry point into the majority of scams, malware infections, and identity thefts.

Think about it: When was the last time you read a story about someone getting hacked because they were brute-forced by a supercomputer? Rarely. But how often do you hear about phishing—when someone clicks on a malicious link and surrenders their information, named because the hacker "fishes" for unsuspecting victims? Constantly. That's because phishing works, and it works because people still click without thinking.

Why Links Are So Dangerous

Links are deceptive by design. The text you see on the screen may not be where the link actually leads. Here are a few examples:

- A link may look like it says www.bankofamerica.com, but hidden underneath, it points to www.bank-secure-login.com—a fake page designed to steal your credentials.
- Shortened links (like bit.ly or tinyurl) hide the destination entirely. Unless you preview them, you have no idea where you're going.

- QR codes, increasingly popular in restaurants and stores, are just visual links. You scan them, and your phone immediately loads a web page. Attackers are now placing fake QR codes on posters, menus, and even parking meters to redirect people to malicious sites.

Attackers love links because they exploit two human tendencies: trust and speed. We trust what looks familiar, and we act quickly when something feels urgent. That's why most phishing messages create a sense of pressure: "Your account will be locked in twenty-four hours—click here to verify." In that panicked moment, your brain bypasses caution and your finger taps the link.

Real-World Examples

- *The package scam*: You get a text: "Your UPS package could not be delivered. Please click here to reschedule." You just ordered something online, so you click. The link leads to a fake UPS login page, which steals your information.
- *The bank alert*: An email arrives claiming to be from your bank. The subject line reads, "Fraudulent activity detected on your account." You panic, click the link, and log in. Except the page isn't your bank—it's a perfect replica built by hackers.
- *The social media message*: A friend's account is compromised, and you receive a message: "Is this you in this video?" with a link. You click it out of curiosity and get prompted to log in to Facebook again. Your credentials are stolen instantly.

These examples aren't rare—they happen millions of times a day. And every successful click means money for the criminals.

What to Do Instead

The safest rule is simple: Never trust a link in an email, text, or message. If you think it might be real, go around it.

- If your bank emails you, don't click the link—open the banking app or type the web address manually.
- If a delivery service texts you, go to their official site directly or use the tracking number in the vendor's app.
- If a friend sends you a suspicious link, call or text them separately to confirm.

Think of it like this: If someone knocked on your door claiming to be from the bank, would you hand them your account details on the spot? Or would you drive to the bank and talk to someone inside? Links are no different—they're digital strangers at your door.

Advanced Defenses

For those ready to go beyond the basics, here are a few extra strategies:

Hover Before You Click

On a computer, hover your mouse over a link before clicking. The actual destination of that link will appear in the bottom corner of your browser. If it doesn't match what you expect, don't click.

Preview Shortened Links

Many services let you add a + to the end of a shortened link to preview it (e.g., bit.ly/example+).

When you add a + to the end of a Bitly link (for example: bit.ly/example+), instead of taking you straight to the destination site, the service shows you a preview page. This page reveals the full URL, when the link was created, and sometimes analytics like how often it's been clicked. It's a quick way to check if the link is pointing somewhere legitimate before exposing your device or network to potential harm.

Attackers often hide malicious links behind shortened URLs because they obscure the true destination. A casual click can lead to phishing pages, drive-by downloads, or credential theft. Teaching people this simple + trick gives them an instant layer of defense without requiring special software. It's a small but powerful digital literacy skill that makes everyday browsing safer.

Not all link shorteners have this + feature, but Bitly and some others do, making it an underused safety tool. For security-conscious users—whether business leaders, parents, or students—this is a practical example of thinking before you click. It ties into the larger theme of your book: that cybersafety isn't always about complex defenses; sometimes it's about knowing small, clever habits that reduce risk.

Use a Link Scanner

Free tools like VirusTotal let you paste in a suspicious link to check it against known malicious domains.

Beware QR Codes

Treat QR codes as suspicious until proven otherwise. If a restaurant menu uses a QR code, confirm it with staff. Don't scan codes from posters or flyers in public spaces.

Enable Browser Protections

Modern browsers like Chrome, Edge, and Safari have built-in phishing and malware protection. Keep them updated so they can warn you if you stumble onto a dangerous site.

Mindset Shift: Retrain Your Clicking Instincts

The hardest part of this habit isn't the technology—it's retraining your instincts. Clicking has become automatic. When you get a message, you want to act fast. To break the habit, build in a pause:

- Read the message carefully.
- Ask yourself, "Why is this urgent? Who benefits from me clicking?"
- Go around the link instead of through it, using the techniques above.

With practice, this becomes second nature—just like looking both ways before crossing the street.

Bottom Line

The majority of cyberattacks start the same way: with a click. Avoid that single action, and you eliminate the attacker's easiest entry point into your life. It's not about being paranoid; it's about being disciplined. The internet is full of doors. Your job is to make sure you don't walk through the wrong one.

HABIT #2: DOWNLOAD APPS DIRECTLY (NEVER FROM MESSAGES)

If Habit #1 was about avoiding the trap of clicking links, Habit #2 is about never letting attackers trick you into installing their software. Because while a malicious link can steal your password, a malicious app can hijack your entire device.

Attackers know how central our phones and computers have become. They're our wallets, calendars, cameras, diaries, and sometimes even our offices. If hackers can convince you to install an app that looks useful but is actually poisoned, they gain access to everything. That's why they constantly send texts, emails, and social messages urging you to "download this app" or "install this update."

The Danger of Downloading from Messages

Imagine you're at work and you receive the following text:

"Your bank account has been locked. Download our security app here to restore access."

It feels urgent, so you tap the link. (Your first mistake! Reread the section above.) The app they want you to download looks professional—it has your bank's logo, colors, and even a login page. But behind the polished design is malware. Instead of protecting your account, it steals your credentials the moment you type them in.

This isn't a hypothetical. Fake banking apps flood app stores every year, often disguised so well that they fool thousands of people. Outside app stores, attackers use direct links in messages to sidestep Apple's and Google's screening process altogether, tricking users into sideloading apps that were never vetted, which means you download the app to your phone outside the app store and bypass whatever security the official store offers you.

The same tactic shows up in emails: "Install this invoice viewer to read your document" or "Update your video player to continue streaming." The bait changes, but the hook is the same—to get you to install from anywhere except the official source.

Why This Works

- *Urgency*: The message creates panic (locked account, missed delivery, expired subscription).
- *Convenience*: They make it one tap away, saving you the trouble of searching for the app yourself.
- *Imitation*: The fake app looks like the real one—right down to the logo and login page.
- *Trust by association*: The message seems to come from a brand you already use, lowering your guard.

The Golden Rule

If an app isn't from the official store or the company's verified website, it doesn't go on your device. Period.

That means the following:

- On mobile, only install from the Apple App Store or Google Play Store.
- On computers, download from the developer's official site, not from "free download" portals or shady mirror sites.
- Never tap a download link in a text, email, or DM, no matter how legitimate it looks.

How to Vet Apps Safely

Even in official stores, there are fake and malicious apps. Criminals sneak in clones by copying names, icons, and descriptions. Do the following to protect yourself:

- *Check the developer name*: Real apps are published by the official company (e.g., "Bank of America Corporation," not "Banking Secure Ltd.").
- *Look at reviews*: Fake apps often have a wave of generic five-star reviews but many detailed one-star warnings.
- *Check update history*: Real apps are updated regularly. If an app hasn't been updated in a year, be wary.
- *Review permissions*: A calculator app doesn't need access to your camera and contacts. Overreaching permissions are a red flag.

The Hidden Risks of Sideloading

On Android, sideloading (installing from outside Google Play) is technically possible. Some users choose to sideload apps for flexibility (or to bypass charges), but it opens the door to enormous risk. Attackers prey on this by disguising malware as popular apps available "for free." Remember, free is never truly free! Unless you are highly technical and know how to verify file signatures, avoid sideloading entirely.

On iPhones, attackers may trick users into installing "enterprise profiles" that allow apps outside the App Store. These profiles are often abused for spyware. If your phone ever prompts you to "trust this profile" for an app that didn't come from the App Store, cancel immediately.

Advanced Defenses

Here are some tips for readers who want to go a step further:

- *Enable app store protections*: Both iOS and Android scan for malicious apps and alert you. Don't disable these settings.
- *Use mobile security tools*: Reputable security apps can scan for rogue apps and warn you if you've installed something suspicious.
- *Separate devices*: Some professionals keep one "clean" phone for banking and personal use and another for experimenting with apps. It's not practical for everyone, but if you rely on your phone for sensitive work, it reduces exposure.
- *Stay informed*: Major banks, carriers, and government agencies publish warnings when fake apps are circulating. A quick search before installing can save you from disaster.

The Mental Shift: Decide to Download

Attackers succeed because they make downloads feel normal. We're conditioned to install apps casually—see it, tap it, done. But the truth is that every app is a guest you invite into your digital house. Would you let a stranger sleep in your spare bedroom just because they looked friendly? Of course not. Yet that's what happens when you install without checking.

From now on, treat every app installation as a decision that deserves scrutiny. Fewer apps, installed more carefully, equals less risk.

Bottom Line

Apps are one of the biggest attack vectors today because they're the keys to your most valuable device—your smartphone. The way to prevent attacks is simple: Only install apps directly from official sources. Don't trust links in texts or emails, don't sideload, and don't ignore red flags like strange permissions or inactive developers.

If you follow this one habit consistently, you'll block one of the most effective paths attackers use to hijack your digital life.

HABIT #3: APP HYGIENE— "AN APP A DAY KEEPS THE EVIL AWAY"

When people think of cyberattacks, they often imagine a hacker breaking through a high-tech firewall. In reality, the weakest link is usually something much simpler: old, never or rarely used apps sitting on your phone or computer.

Every app you install is a doorway into your digital life. Some doors are well built, locked, and monitored. Others are flimsy, left ajar, or forgotten altogether. The more apps you have, the more doors you expose—and the more chances attackers have to walk in.

That's why app hygiene—keeping only what you need and removing what you don't—is one of the most underrated but powerful cybersecurity habits you can adopt.

The Hidden Dangers of Extra Apps

Here's the problem: Apps don't just sit quietly when you're not using them. Many run in the background, collecting data, tracking your activity, or "phoning home" to their servers. Some request permissions they don't really need, like access to your microphone, contacts, or location. And others, especially if they've been abandoned by their developers, become outdated and vulnerable to known exploits.

Consider this real-world scenario: A fitness app you downloaded two years ago still sits on your phone. You don't use it anymore, but it still has permission to access your GPS, health data, and contacts. The developer stopped updating it last year. Hackers discover a flaw in the app's code, and because you never removed it, your phone is now at risk—even though you haven't opened the app in months.

This isn't rare. Many high-profile breaches have occurred through "forgotten" apps that remained on devices with excessive permissions.

Why We Keep Too Many Apps

Most of us are guilty of app hoarding. We download a new game, a coupon app, or a travel tool for a single trip, and then we forget about it. Over time, our devices become cluttered with apps we don't use.

Why do we keep them?

- *Convenience*: "I might use it again one day."
- *Laziness*: Deleting takes effort, and we underestimate the risk.
- *FOMO*: We don't want to lose the content, progress, or data inside the app.

But here's the truth: Unused apps are liabilities, not assets. Every unnecessary app increases your attack surface—the number of ways hackers can get to you.

The "App a Day" Challenge

To simplify app hygiene, I created a phrase I use in my talks: "An app a day keeps evil away."

Here's how it works:

- Each day, delete one app you don't use.
- If that sounds like too much, aim for one app a week.
- In a month or two, you'll dramatically reduce the number of potential vulnerabilities on your device.

Start with apps you haven't opened in the last thirty days. If you haven't used it in a month, you probably don't need it.

How to Audit Your Apps

Check Usage

Both iOS and Android show you when you last used each app. If it's been months, delete it.

On iPhone (iOS):

Go to Settings > General > iPhone Storage. You'll see a list of all your apps, sorted by storage use, with a note under each one showing when you last used it. If an app hasn't been touched in months, it's time to delete it—or at least offload it to free up space and reduce risk.

On Android:

Open Settings > Apps (or Apps & Notifications). Select See All Apps to view the list, then tap the three-dot menu and sort by Last Used. Any apps you haven't opened in months are candidates for removal.

Review Permissions

Look at which apps can access your location, microphone, camera, contacts, and photos. Ask yourself, "Does this app really need this access?" If not, revoke permissions—or delete the app.

On iPhone (iOS):

Open Settings > Privacy & Security. You'll see categories like Location Services, Contacts, Photos, Camera, and Microphone. Tap each one to view which apps have access, and switch off any that don't need it.

On Android:

Go to Settings > Privacy > Permission Manager (sometimes called App Permissions depending on your device). Here you will find lists for Location, Camera, Microphone, Contacts, and Photos/Media. Open each category to see which apps have access, and adjust permissions.

Update Survivors

For the apps you keep, ensure they're updated. Old versions are a hacker's playground.

Remove Linked Accounts: Before deleting, disconnect the app from any accounts (Google, Facebook, Apple ID). Otherwise, it may keep some level of access.

Google:

Go to myaccount.google.com > Security > Third-party apps with account access. Review the list, and click on any app you no longer use. Select Remove Access to disconnect it from your Google account.

Facebook:

Open Settings & Privacy > Settings > Security and Login > Apps and Websites. You'll see apps that are connected to your Facebook login. Select the app, and choose Remove to cut the link.

Apple ID:

On iPhone, open Settings > [your name] > Password & Security > Apps Using Apple ID. This shows all apps linked through "Sign in with Apple." Tap any app you no longer use, and choose Stop Using Apple ID.

If you delete an app without disconnecting it, the app may still retain a connection to your personal data through your Google, Facebook, or Apple accounts. Disconnecting ensures the app is fully cut off and can no longer pull information in the background. This step locks the door behind you when you leave.

Advanced Practices

For readers ready to take app hygiene seriously, here are some professional-level tips:

- *Separate profiles*: Use one browser or phone profile for sensitive activities like banking and another for casual apps. This limits what a compromised app can touch.
- *Limit background data*: Many phones let you restrict apps from running in the background. Apply this to apps you don't fully trust but still want to keep.
- *Beware browser extensions*: They are apps, too, often with broad permissions. Keep only what you truly use.
- *Check developer activity*: If an app hasn't been updated in a year or two, think twice about keeping it.

Abandoned apps often have unpatched security flaws.

- *Schedule cleanups*: Put a reminder on your calendar every month to review and clean out apps.

Mindset Shift: Fewer Apps = More Control

Think of your device like your house. Would you hand out spare keys to a hundred acquaintances and then hope none of them abuse your trust? That's what you're doing when you install dozens of apps without reviewing them.

Every app you remove is one less key floating around. Every permission you revoke is one less window left open. The goal isn't to eliminate all apps—it's to keep your circle small, intentional, and trustworthy.

Bottom Line

App hygiene isn't glamorous, but it's effective. By deleting what you don't use and controlling permissions on what you keep, you shrink your digital attack surface and give attackers fewer options. Remember, every app is a potential door. The fewer doors you have, the safer your digital house becomes.

So take the challenge: one app a day, or at least a handful a week. In forty-five days, you'll look at your device and realize you're not just safer—you're faster, lighter, and in control.

HABIT #4: STRONG, UNIQUE PASSWORDS (WITH A PASSWORD MANAGER)

If there's one thing hackers love more than anything, it's people who reuse their passwords. Having weak or recycled passwords is like leaving the same key under the doormat of every house you've ever lived in. Once someone finds it, they can stroll into all of them at will.

And here's the truth: Most hacks you hear about aren't some genius coder breaking impossible encryption. They're simply criminals logging in with stolen or guessed passwords. It's boring, but it works—and it works because people don't take password habits seriously.

Why Passwords Still Matter

You've probably heard, "Passwords are outdated." And yes, the future is moving toward biometrics and passwordless systems. But for now, passwords remain the first line of defense for almost every account you own—email, banking, social media, health care, cloud storage.

The weakness isn't the concept of passwords. It's the way people use them:

- Reusing the same password across multiple accounts
- Choosing simple phrases like "password123" or "letmein"
- Using personal details like birthdays, pets, or favorite teams—things that can be guessed from social media

Attackers thrive on this. Once they get one working

combination of your email and password from a breach, they try it everywhere else. This is called credential stuffing. If you've reused that password on more than one account, they're in.

Why Complexity Alone Isn't Enough

A lot of advice says, "Make your password long and complex." That's true, but complexity alone won't save you if you reuse the same password across sites. Imagine you create the world's strongest password—"8d!Q9p$1Xz#Wv"—and then use it for email, Facebook, and online banking. If any one of those sites is breached, criminals test it everywhere else.

The only real solution is having a unique password for every account. That way, a single breach doesn't cause a chain reaction.

Why You Need a Password Manager

Here's the pushback I usually hear: "But I can't remember hundreds of unique passwords!" Exactly. That's why you need a password manager.

A password manager is like a vault. It stores all your credentials in encrypted form and unlocks them with a single master password. From there, it can do the following:

- Generate random, strong passwords you don't have to memorize.
- Autofill credentials in apps and browsers, saving you time.
- Warn you if you're reusing or creating weak passwords.
- Alert you if any of your credentials show up in a breach.

Popular managers include 1Password, Bitwarden, and Dashlane. Browsers like Chrome and Safari also offer password management, but a dedicated tool gives you more control, more features, and better alerts.

How to Build Strong Password Habits

Lock Down Your Email First

Your primary email is the most critical account you own because it's the recovery point for everything else. If someone compromises it, they can reset passwords to all your accounts. Make this your strongest, most protected login.

Upgrade Critical Accounts

Next, secure accounts tied to money, identity, or data: banks, health care portals, password manager, cloud storage, tax services, and social media platforms you rely on for work.

Embrace Passphrases

Instead of random gibberish, use a combination of unrelated words with symbols or numbers sprinkled in. Examples include "SilverBanana!Train47" or "Ocean+Desk%Planet2024." These are easier to remember yet still strong.

Enable Breach Alerts

Many managers and services now check your credentials against known breach databases. If your login shows up, change it immediately.

Use Multi-Factor Authentication

Even the best password can be stolen. MFA adds a second layer—like a one-time code, authenticator app, or hardware key. If someone tries to log in with your password, they're blocked without the second factor.

Security Questions: The Silent Weakness

Many accounts still use security questions as backups. The problem? Most answers can be guessed or researched. Your mother's maiden name, the city you were born, your first pet's name—all this is on Facebook or in public records.

The fix? Treat security questions like extra passwords. Don't answer them truthfully—answer them randomly, and store the responses in your password manager. If a site asks for your first school, your answer might be "OrangeRiver99$Tree." Nobody can guess that.

Advanced Protection: Hardware Keys

For your most sensitive accounts—email, banking, password manager itself—consider using a hardware security key like a YubiKey. This small device plugs into your computer or taps against your phone to confirm your login. Even if an attacker has your password, they can't log in without the physical key in your possession.

Mindset Shift: Offloading the Mental Load

We treat passwords as chores, but they're really the locks on our lives. You wouldn't use the same key for your house, car, office, and safe-deposit box. So why use the same password everywhere?

Password managers shift the mental load. Instead of juggling dozens of fragile locks, you manage one strong master key, and the system takes care of the rest.

Bottom Line

Passwords are still the front door of cybersecurity. Weak, reused ones are like leaving that door wide open. Strong, unique ones—stored and managed properly—turn it into a steel barrier.

So commit to this habit: Every account gets its own password, managed by a vault. Lock down your email first, then your finances, and then everything else. Use MFA for extra protection. And never tell the truth on security questions. It may feel like extra work in the beginning, but once the manager is set up, your digital life actually becomes easier. And safer.

HABIT #5: KEEP SOFTWARE UPDATED (CLOSE THE DOORS ATTACKERS ALREADY KNOW ABOUT)

If there's one habit that feels boring but can save your online life, it's this one: Keep your software updated. Updates may not sound glamorous, but in the world of cybersecurity, they are the equivalent of not only locking your doors but fixing your broken locks.

Most people think of updates as annoying interruptions—pop-ups at the worst possible moment, nagging notifications, or slow reboots when you're in a hurry. But here's the truth: Every time you ignore an update, you're leaving a door wide open, and attackers know it's unlocked.

Why Updates Matter More than You Think

Every piece of software—your phone's operating system, your computer's browser, your favorite apps—has flaws. Developers fix those flaws by releasing updates. The moment an update is published, attackers reverse engineer it to understand what was wrong in the previous version. Then they immediately begin scanning the internet for anyone who hasn't updated yet.

Think of it like this: The update is a patch on a hole in your roof. If you don't get one, you'll get soaked.

Real-World Examples

- *WannaCry ransomware* (2017): This global ransomware attack hit over two hundred thousand computers in more than 150 countries. The exploit it used had already been patched by Microsoft months earlier. Victims weren't hacked because the patch didn't exist—they were hacked because they hadn't installed it.
- *Equifax breach* (2017): Hackers stole personal information on nearly 150 million people. The vulnerability they exploited had a patch available two months before the attack. But the company hadn't updated the software in time.
- *Zoom vulnerabilities* (2020): During the pandemic, millions rushed to use Zoom for work and school. Hackers quickly discovered flaws in older versions that let them crash meetings or even hijack devices. Updates fixed these holes, but anyone who didn't install them was exposed.

The pattern is clear: The danger isn't unknown flaws—it's known flaws left unpatched.

The Psychology of Delaying Updates

So why do people resist updating?

- *Inconvenience*: Nobody likes stopping what they're doing to reboot.
- *Fear of change*: Updates sometimes move buttons or add features, and people don't want to relearn.
- *Complacency*: "It won't happen to me."
- *Laziness*: We think we'll "do it later," but later rarely comes.

Attackers count on this behavior. They don't have to invent new exploits—they just wait for you to procrastinate.

Building the Update Habit

The solution is simple: Treat updates like brushing your teeth. It's not exciting, but if you skip it, decay sets in.

Here's how to make it practical:

Enable Automatic Updates

- On smartphones, turn on automatic updates for apps and system software.
- On computers, let Windows Update or macOS Software Update run automatically.
- For browsers like Chrome, Edge, and Firefox,

updates usually happen automatically in the background—just restart the browser regularly.

Restart Regularly

Many updates only finish installing after a reboot. If you never restart, you may think you're updated when you're not. A weekly restart is a healthy baseline.

Prioritize Browsers

Most attacks happen through the internet. Keeping your browser updated is one of the single most powerful security moves you can make.

Update Your Router

Your home Wi-Fi router is the front gate to your entire digital life. It also runs software (firmware) that needs updates. Log in every few months, and check for patches. Change the default admin password while you're at it.

Retire Abandoned Software

Some programs stop receiving updates altogether when developers move on. These "end-of-life" apps are permanent weak spots. Replace them with supported alternatives.

Advanced Practices

Here are some tips for those who want to go further:

- *Use patch management tools*: This is particularly important if you manage multiple computers (especially in a small business). These tools automate updates across all machines.

- *Subscribe to vendor alerts*: Apple, Microsoft, and Google publish security bulletins. Knowing what's being fixed gives you a sense of urgency.
- *Segment critical devices*: For ultrasensitive tasks (like banking), use a device that only runs updated essentials—no extra apps, no games, no clutter.

Mindset Shift: Updates Are Shields

Updates aren't nuisances; they're shields. Each one is a bandage over a wound, a lock on a door, a repair on your digital foundation. Skipping them doesn't just leave you vulnerable—it makes you an easy target, because attackers know exactly who hasn't patched.

Imagine if a car manufacturer recalled a faulty brake system and offered you a free repair. Would you ignore it? Of course not. That's what software updates are: free repairs for defects that could crash your system.

Bottom Line

Most major cyberattacks succeed not because of brilliant hackers but because of lazy updating. The fix is free, simple, and available—you just have to apply it.

So commit to this: Enable automatic updates, restart weekly, and never ignore update prompts. When software tells you it's time, it's not nagging—it's protecting. By making updates a habit instead of an afterthought, you close the very doors attackers depend on.

HABIT #6: RECOGNIZE AND RESPOND TO SUSPICIOUS ACTIVITY

Even if you follow every cybersecurity best practice, no system is perfect. Sooner or later, something suspicious may slip through: a strange login alert, an email you didn't send, or an unexplained charge on your credit card. The difference between a nuisance and a nightmare often comes down to how quickly you recognize the signs and how quickly you respond.

In cybersecurity, time is everything. Hackers count on hesitation. The sooner you act, the less damage they can do.

Why Early Recognition Matters

Imagine a thief breaking into a house. If the homeowner walks in during the break-in, the thief grabs a few things and runs. If the break-in goes unnoticed for days, the thief can empty the place. The same principle applies online. If you notice a breach immediately, you can cut off the attacker before they dig in. If you don't notice for weeks, they may have drained accounts, stolen identities, or planted back doors you'll never fully detect.

Many of the worst data breaches started small: a single compromised account that wasn't noticed for months. By the time anyone paid attention, the attackers had already spread everywhere.

Common Warning Signs

You don't need to be a security expert to spot suspicious activity. Most signs are obvious if you train yourself to pay attention. Here are red flags you should never ignore:

Unfamiliar Login Alerts

If you receive an email saying, "New login from an unknown device or location," take it seriously. Even if the login was "blocked," it means someone has your password.

Emails or Messages You Didn't Send

If friends report strange messages from you—or you see copies of emails in your sent folder you didn't write—your account may be compromised.

Unexpected Password Reset Notifications

If you get alerts about password resets you didn't initiate, someone is trying to take control of your account.

Mysterious App Installations

If new apps, browser extensions, or toolbars appear that you don't remember installing, that's a red flag.

Pop-Ups and Sluggish Devices

Excessive pop-ups, slow performance, or programs crashing unexpectedly may signal malware.

Strange Bank Activity

Small, unexplained charges on your card are often "test" transactions by criminals. If they go unnoticed, larger charges will follow.

Locked-Out Accounts

If you suddenly can't log in to an account and your password no longer works, assume it's compromised.

The Right Way to Respond

When you see suspicious activity, panic is your worst enemy. The best response is calm, structured action. Here's the playbook:

Change Your Passwords Immediately

Start with your email account. Since email is the hub for password resets, locking it down first prevents further damage. Then change passwords for any other affected accounts.

Enable or Strengthen MFA

If you haven't already, turn on multi-factor authentication. If you already had it, switch from SMS codes to an authenticator app or hardware key.

Log Out of All Sessions

Most services let you log out of all active sessions. This kicks out the intruder even if they still have your password.

Scan for Malware

Use reputable security software to scan your device. If the scan comes back clean but issues persist, consider a full backup and reinstall.

Check Account Access

Many services (Google, Facebook, Microsoft) allow you to review connected apps and devices. Revoke anything you don't recognize.

Contact Your Bank or Provider

If money is involved, call your bank immediately. Cancel cards, reverse charges, and set up alerts for future transactions.

Document Everything

Write down the suspicious activity, times, and actions taken. This helps if you need to escalate to customer support or law enforcement.

Real-World Example

A colleague once noticed a three-dollar charge on his credit card from a company he didn't recognize. It seemed too small to worry about, so he ignored it. Two weeks later, his card was maxed out with fraudulent charges totaling thousands of dollars.

That three dollars was a test transaction. Criminals often make tiny charges first to confirm that the card is active. If it slips past unnoticed, they go big. Had he acted immediately, he could have canceled the card before the damage escalated.

Advanced Tips

Here are some tips for those who want an extra layer of protection:

- *Set up alerts*: Most banks and online services allow you to receive instant notifications for logins, payments, or changes. Turn them on.
- *Use account dashboards*: Check "last login" and device history regularly, especially for critical accounts like email and banking.
- *Segment your email*: Consider having a separate email account solely for financial and sensitive accounts. Fewer connections mean fewer chances of compromise.
- *Don't ignore "blocked" login attempts*: Even if a login was stopped, it means your password is out there. Rotate it.

Mindset Shift: No Risk for Overreacting

Most people ignore red flags because they hope they're false alarms. But in cybersecurity, overreacting costs little—while underreacting can be catastrophic. Clicking a few extra buttons to change a password or call your bank is a small inconvenience compared to rebuilding your identity after a full compromise.

Think of suspicious activity like smelling smoke in your house. You don't assume it's nothing—you check until you're sure.

Bottom Line

Suspicious activity is not something to "wait and see." Every minute counts. If you respond immediately—changing passwords, enabling MFA, revoking access, and contacting your bank—you can limit damage to a blip. If you ignore the signs, that blip becomes a disaster.

Make this a habit: See something; do something. Treat every unusual login, reset, or charge as serious until proven otherwise. The faster you act, the less they win.

HABIT #7: REGAINING YOUR ONLINE IDENTITY AFTER BEING COMPROMISED

No matter how careful you are, the reality is that sometimes an attacker still slips through. Maybe you missed an update, clicked the wrong link at two in the morning, or a reused password from years ago finally caught up with you. Suddenly, you find yourself locked out of your email, your friends are receiving strange messages from you, or worse, money is missing from your accounts.

This is every internet user's nightmare—but it's not the end of the world. The difference between permanent damage and a temporary scare comes down to how quickly and how methodically you respond.

Think of this like a fire drill. You don't want to figure it out on the spot, in the panic of the flames. You want a plan you can follow step-by-step.

Step 1: Regain Control of Your Primary Email

Your email account is the central hub of your online identity. It's the key that unlocks password resets for nearly every other service—banks, shopping sites, cloud storage, and social media. That makes it the first target for attackers and the first place you need to regain control.

- *Change the password immediately*: Do this from a clean device (not one you think may be infected).
- *Enable MFA if you haven't already*: Use an authenticator app or hardware key, not SMS if possible.
- *Check recovery options*: Make sure your recovery email and phone number are correct and belong to you—not swapped out by the attacker.
- *Log out of all sessions*: Many email services let you force a logout across all devices. This kicks the attacker out even if they still know your password.

If you can't regain access, contact the email provider's recovery team immediately. Most large platforms have dedicated processes for compromised accounts.

Step 2: Lock Down Your Finances

If attackers have access to your email, they can often access your financial accounts. Move quickly:

- *Contact your bank or credit card company*: Report the compromise, and freeze accounts if necessary. Most banks can issue new cards quickly.
- *Set up transaction alerts*: Get notified instantly of any charges or withdrawals.
- *Review your statements carefully*: Look for both large and small unfamiliar charges. Criminals often "test" cards with tiny amounts before going bigger.
- *Consider a credit freeze*: Placing a freeze with major credit bureaus (Experian, Equifax, TransUnion) prevents criminals from opening new accounts in your name.

Step 3: Evict the Attacker's Footholds

Hackers are sneaky. Even after you change passwords, they may leave behind hidden access points.

- *Check connected apps*: Services like Google, Microsoft, and Facebook let you review which apps and devices are linked to your account. Revoke anything suspicious or outdated.
- *Rotate access tokens*: If you've linked accounts together (for example, using Google or Facebook to log in to another website or app), update those logins too.
- *Check for forwarding rules*: Some attackers set up

email rules to silently forward your messages to them. Delete any you don't recognize.

This step is often overlooked—and it's where many people get rehacked even after "recovering."

Step 4: Clean and Rebuild Your Devices

If your device is infected, attackers may still be watching everything you type. Don't assume recovery is complete until your hardware is secure.

- Run a full malware scan with reputable security software.
- Check start-up items for unfamiliar programs.
- Remove shady extensions from your browsers.
- If problems persist, back up important files and do a full reinstall. Start fresh with a clean operating system.

Yes, doing all this can be inconvenient. But remember, convenience now is nothing compared to the pain of being compromised again tomorrow.

Step 5: Inform and Protect Your Network

Compromises don't just affect you—they can spill over to your family, friends, and coworkers.

- *Tell your contacts*: If your email or social media was used to send scam messages, notify people so they don't fall for it.

- *Post a short notice on compromised social accounts once you regain control*: "My account was hacked. Please ignore any messages sent between [dates]."
- *Educate your family*: If one household account is hacked, it's common for criminals to pivot to others. Share your recovery process so your family members can check their accounts too.

Step 6: Monitor for Fallout

Recovery doesn't end when you reset your password. Attackers may try again—or sell your information to others.

- Watch your inbox for suspicious password reset attempts.
- Check your credit report for new accounts or loans you didn't authorize.
- Stay alert for phishing attempts pretending to be "support" offering to help you fix your account.

This is often the second wave of the attack—criminals know you're vulnerable and stressed, so they target you again.

Step 7: Learn and Fortify

Every compromise is painful, but it's also an opportunity to strengthen your defenses. Ask yourself the following questions:

- "What was the entry point?" (A reused password? A missed update? Clicking a link?)
- "How can I prevent it from happening again?"

- "Which habits from this book can I implement now to reduce risk?"

Document your process. The next time you see warning signs, you'll be able to react twice as fast.

Mindset Shift: Take Back Control

Being compromised doesn't mean you failed. It means you're human. Hackers rely on shame and fear to keep victims quiet—but recovery is about taking back control. The key is to stop thinking, "This shouldn't happen to me" and start thinking, "When it happens, I'll know what to do."

Bottom Line

Regaining your online identity after a compromise is about moving quickly, methodically, and decisively. Secure your email, lock down finances, evict the attacker's back doors, clean your devices, and monitor for fallout.

The most important part? Learn from it. Every attack survived makes you stronger, more aware, and less likely to fall for the next one. Think of it as fireproofing your house after a scare—you don't just rebuild; you rebuild smarter.

HABIT #8: EMBRACE AI SAFELY—MAKE IT YOUR BODYGUARD, NOT YOUR LIABILITY

When most people hear the terms *AI* and *cybersecurity*, their first thought is fear. They've read the headlines about AI-generated phishing emails, deepfake scams, or automated hacking tools that can break into accounts faster than any human. And it's true—attackers are weaponizing AI in powerful new ways.

But here's the part most people miss: AI can protect you too. In fact, many of the most effective security tools available right now are powered by AI. The difference comes down to whether you ignore it—or embrace it.

This habit isn't about avoiding AI. It's about learning to make AI your digital bodyguard instead of your digital enemy.

Why AI Matters for Everyday Users

Think about your daily online life. You get dozens of emails, texts, and notifications. Some are real; some are scams. Could you manually inspect each one? Maybe for a while, but over time fatigue sets in—and fatigue is what attackers rely on.

AI doesn't get tired. It doesn't miss patterns. It can analyze millions of emails, logins, and transactions in the time it takes you to sip a coffee. That makes it an incredible ally if you're willing to turn on and trust the right features.

How AI Already Protects You (Even If You Don't Realize It)

Email and Messaging Filters

Gmail, Outlook, and iCloud all use AI to scan messages for phishing attempts. They don't just look at keywords—they analyze sender behavior, link patterns, and even writing style. That's why most scams never even hit your inbox.

Fraud Detection in Banking

Ever had your bank freeze your card after an unusual transaction? That's AI at work. These systems study your normal spending and flag anything out of character—like a gas station charge across the country or repeated small test charges.

Login Monitoring

Platforms like Google and Microsoft use AI to recognize unusual login attempts. If you normally log in from Virginia and suddenly someone tries from Russia, the system knows it's suspicious and challenges it with extra verification.

Malware and Virus Detection

Modern antivirus tools no longer rely just on "signatures" of known malware. They use AI to spot unusual behavior—like a program suddenly encrypting hundreds of files—and stop it in real time.

How You Can Use AI More Intentionally

While some protections run quietly in the background, others require you to enable or adopt them. Here's where you can take action:

Password Managers with AI

Many password managers now include AI that scans your vault of passwords for weak, reused, or compromised ones. They can even suggest stronger replacements.

AI-Powered Identity Monitoring

Services like Aura, IdentityForce, and others use AI to scan the dark web for your personal information. If your email, phone number, or SSN appears in stolen data, you'll get an alert before criminals use it.

Smart Privacy Coaches

Some apps now review your social media profiles and privacy settings, warning you if you're oversharing details like your home address in a photo's metadata.

Deepfake Detection Tools

Free and paid tools are emerging that use AI to analyze suspicious videos or voice recordings, helping you verify whether they're real or manipulated.

AI Scam Filters

Certain mobile apps can intercept suspicious texts and calls, analyzing them with AI to warn you if they're likely to be scams.

The Risks of Misusing AI

Of course, like any tool, AI comes with risks if you're careless. Public AI chatbots aren't meant to handle your sensitive data. Never paste passwords, confidential client information, or financial details into them. Assume that whatever you type could be stored or analyzed later.

Instead, use enterprise or privacy-first AI tools when dealing with sensitive tasks. And always balance automation with awareness—AI can help you, but you still need to pay attention to the alerts and warnings it gives you.

Advanced Tips for Power Users

- *Enable all built-in protections on the apps and platforms you already use*: Many platforms ship with strong AI security features, but they're not always on by default. Go into your account or device security settings and max them out.

- *Layer tools*: Don't rely on one AI product alone. Use email filters, a password manager, and financial fraud alerts together.
- *Test yourself*: Ask an AI to generate a phishing email based on what you share publicly. Seeing how convincing it looks will teach you what to lock down.
- *Stay updated*: AI tools evolve quickly. Subscribe to updates from your password manager, bank, or security app to learn about new features.

Mindset Shift: AI as Security Analyst

Attackers will use AI whether you like it or not. The only real question is whether you'll use it too. Think of AI as a security analyst who works 24-7 on your behalf. It never sleeps, it never blinks, and it can see patterns you'll never spot on your own. But like any analyst, it needs you to listen. When it raises a flag, take it seriously.

Bottom Line

AI is already shaping the future of cybersecurity, but it's not just for hackers and big companies—it's for you. By adopting AI-driven tools for passwords, monitoring, scam detection, and fraud prevention, you put a powerful shield between yourself and the attackers.

So embrace AI safely. Turn on the protections you already have, add tools where they make sense, and keep sensitive data out of public AI systems. Done right, AI becomes your bodyguard—standing between you and the endless stream of threats that fill the digital world.

BRINGING THE HABITS TOGETHER

These eight habits are not "nice to haves." They are a living system. You go around the link instead of through it. You install from trusted places or not at all. You trim your apps to what you truly need. You let a password manager do the heavy lifting and pair it with MFA. You update like it's oxygen. You watch for signals and respond quickly. If something slips through, you recover methodically. And now, you enlist AI—already embedded in the tools you use—to shoulder some of the load.

Here's how you can make it all practical in your day-to-day life:

- *Daily*: No impulsive clicks; use official apps only; pay attention for anything that seems "off."
- *Weekly*: Updates; purge apps as much as you can; quick glances at recent logins and transactions.
- *Monthly*: Permissions audit; password manager health check; backup test; router firmware check.
- *Quarterly*: Account access review (OAuth tokens, connected apps); recovery info refresh (phone, email, trusted contacts); financial statement sweep for "tiny" fraud.

Small, repeatable steps beat heroic, once-a-year overhauls. That's how you win: quietly, consistently, with habits that don't break when life gets busy.

You don't need perfection. You need a process you'll actually follow. Follow the eight habits in this chapter, and you'll move yourself out of the easy-target category—right where attackers least want you to be.

LIVE WITH CONFIDENCE

By now you've seen that cybersecurity isn't about memorizing complex jargon or buying expensive tools—it's about building simple, repeatable habits. Just like brushing your teeth or locking your doors, the small things you do every day are what keep you safe in the long run.

Think about the eight habits we've covered:

- *Never click on a link*: Go around, not through. It only takes one wrong click to give an attacker the keys to your life.
- *Download apps directly*: If it didn't come from the official store or verified site, it doesn't belong on your device.
- *Practice app hygiene*: An app a day keeps the evil away. Every deletion shrinks your attack surface.
- *Use strong, unique passwords with a manager*: One password per account, managed by a vault, backed by MFA.
- *Keep software updated*: Updates aren't nuisances—they're shields. Install them fast.
- *Recognize and respond to suspicious activity*: The faster you act, the less attackers win.
- *Regain identity methodically if compromised*: Don't panic. Secure email first, lock finances, evict footholds, clean devices, and monitor for fallout.
- *Embrace AI safely*: Attackers use it against you—make sure you're using it for yourself too.

On their own, each habit blocks a major attack vector. Together, they form a system—a set of routines that hardens your defenses without overwhelming your daily life. You don't need to do everything at once. Start with the habit that feels most urgent—maybe deleting unused apps, enabling MFA, or setting up a password manager—and build from there.

The point isn't perfection. The point is progress. Every good habit you adopt moves you out of the "easy target" category. And that's the secret: Attackers don't go after the hardest prey—they go after the easiest. If you make yourself harder to hack than the next person, most criminals will move on.

Cybersecurity doesn't have to be complicated. It doesn't even have to take more than a few minutes a day. It just requires the same thing all good habits require: consistency.

So, as you close this chapter, remember this: You don't need to be a tech genius to stay safe online. You just need to treat your digital life with the same care you give your physical one. Lock your doors, check your windows, and build routines that protect you without thought.

When you do, you stop living in fear of cyberattacks—and start living with the confidence that you're in control of your digital world.

KEY TAKEAWAYS

- ☐ Go around, not through. Never click a link you didn't initiate; use official apps and typed-in sites.
- ☐ Install clean. Do so only from app stores or verified vendor sites; no downloads from messages, pop-ups, or QR posters.
- ☐ Reduce the surface that can be hacked. An app a day keeps the evil away—delete what you don't use; revoke stale permissions and account connections.
- ☐ Unique + MFA. Use a password manager for every login and an authenticator or hardware key for the important stuff.
- ☐ Patch fast. Turn auto-updates on; do browsers first: reboot weekly, router firmware quarterly.
- ☐ Respond fast. Isolate; secure email first; notify bank; revoke rogue access; document.
- ☐ Recover methodically. Identity → finances → devices → communications → lessons learned.
- ☐ Let AI help. Enable AI defenses you already own; pick reputable tools; keep sensitive data out of public AI; let AI coach your habits.

CONCLUSION

SECURING CYBERSPACE—WHAT'S NEXT?

A few years ago, I met a family in Texas who had just gone through a cyber nightmare. Their teenage daughter had her Instagram account hacked, and the attacker used it to message her friends, asking for money and personal information. At the same time, the father received phishing emails pretending to be from his bank. Within a week, the family's confidence in technology was shaken. They felt violated, overwhelmed, and unsure of what to do.

But instead of giving up, they decided to take action together. They treated cybersecurity not as a technical problem for "IT people" but as a family habit—just like wearing seat belts or locking doors at night. They went through every device in the house, deleting unused apps and setting up password managers. They enabled two-factor authentication on all accounts. The kids agreed to make their social media accounts private. They even scheduled a "cyber checkup" every Sunday evening to update software, review bank alerts, and talk about anything unusual online.

The result? In a matter of weeks, they went from victims to defenders. The attacks didn't stop—the scams and phishing emails still came—but the family had built habits that made them resilient. They no longer felt powerless. They felt in control.

That family's story is a reminder of what this entire book has been about. Cybersecurity isn't a mystical force controlled by governments or giant corporations. It's something that begins in our homes, our offices, our communities. It's about awareness, habits, and the willingness to take action. And just as that family discovered, the future of cybersecurity won't be built only in Washington, Silicon Valley, or Wall Street. It will be built by all of us—together.

LOOKING BACK: WHAT WE'VE LEARNED

Over the last chapters, we've explored the everyday realities of digital life and the practical steps anyone can take to stay safe. Some of the lessons were simple, like never clicking on suspicious links or keeping your software updated. Others required a little more effort, like embracing password managers, practicing app hygiene, or learning how to recognize deepfakes and social engineering scams.

The key theme throughout has been this: Cybersecurity is not about tools; it's about habits.

- Your smartphone is not automatically safe; it becomes safe when you manage apps carefully, review permissions, and use secure payment methods.
- Your computer is not invincible; it becomes resilient when you update it, avoid shady downloads, and learn to spot suspicious emails.
- The cloud is not secure by default; it becomes secure when you use encryption, two-factor authentication, and responsible sharing practices.
- Social media isn't dangerous on its own; it becomes dangerous when you overshare, ignore privacy settings, or fall for impersonation scams.

And woven through it all has been the role of artificial intelligence—sometimes as the attacker's weapon, sometimes as your ally. AI can clone voices, write convincing phishing emails, or scan billions of accounts for weaknesses. But AI also powers your email filters, fraud detection, and password managers. The future will be shaped by this dual-use reality.

Cybersecurity is no longer about asking if you'll be targeted. It's about how prepared you'll be when you are.

LOOKING FORWARD: THE CHANGING LANDSCAPE

The digital world is not slowing down. If anything, the pace of change is accelerating. That means the habits you've built through this book aren't the end of the journey—they're the foundation for what comes next.

Here are some of the key trends shaping the future of cybersecurity:

AI Everywhere

This book has only scratched the surface of what artificial intelligence can do. Attackers are already using AI to generate personalized scams at scale. Imagine receiving a phishing email written not in broken English but in flawless language, referencing details of your life pulled from your public posts. Or a phone call in the exact voice and cadence of your spouse asking you to wire money. That's the reality AI makes possible.

But AI is also our strongest defense. It can analyze login patterns, detect anomalies in milliseconds, and scan billions of transactions for fraud. In the future, your devices will come with

AI "copilots" that continuously monitor your activity, silently shielding you from attacks you never even see.

The challenge will be learning to trust and guide these systems while still ultimately relying on human judgment.

The Expanding Internet of Things

Our homes, cars, and even appliances are now connected to the internet. That means every thermostat, baby monitor, and smart speaker is a potential entry point for attackers. The more connected our lives become, the more we must pay attention to the basics—changing default passwords, updating firmware, and segmenting devices on our networks.

Deepfakes and Disinformation

The rise of deepfakes signals a new era where seeing is no longer believing. Criminals and propagandists alike will use AI-generated content to manipulate opinions, coerce individuals, and destabilize trust in institutions. Combating this will require both technological tools and cultural literacy—learning to question, verify, and cross-check information before we accept it as true.

Cybersecurity as a Shared Responsibility

Just as public health depends on everyone washing their hands, cybersecurity will increasingly depend on collective action. When one person falls for a phishing email at work, the whole company can be compromised. When one student overshares on social media, their entire family can be put at risk. The future of security will be built not only on individual habits but on community-wide awareness and responsibility.

Policy and Regulation Catching Up

Governments worldwide are struggling to keep up with the pace of change. Cybercrime is global, but laws are local. We will see more attempts at international cooperation, new regulations on AI, and stricter requirements for companies to protect consumer data. Citizens will play a role in holding leaders accountable and pushing for smarter, more modern policies.

HOW INDIVIDUALS CAN STAY INFORMED AND INVOLVED

The habits you've built are your armor. But staying safe also requires keeping an eye on the horizon. Here's how to do it without feeling overwhelmed:

Follow Trusted Sources

Subscribe to cybersecurity newsletters or podcasts that break down complex issues in plain language. Avoid sensational headlines; look for sources that focus on practical advice.

Treat Learning as Ongoing

Just as you update your software, update your knowledge. Set aside a little time each month to read about new scams or tools. Think of it as a "cyber checkup."

Practice Digital Leadership at Home

Teach your kids, parents, or friends the basics you've learned here. Cybersecurity spreads like any habit—through example.

Engage with Your Community

Schools, workplaces, and local organizations all benefit from more cyber awareness. Share what you know. Offer to run a simple "digital safety night" at your child's school, or talk about secure habits at work.

Stay Skeptical but Empowered

The digital world will always evolve. Instead of fearing every new technology, approach it with cautious optimism. Ask, "How can I use this safely? What protections should I enable? How can I make this tool work for me, not against me?"

BUILDING A MORE CYBER-AWARE SOCIETY

Ultimately, the future of cybersecurity isn't just about protecting ourselves individually—it's about building a more cyber-aware society. Imagine if digital literacy were taught alongside reading and math. Imagine if communities viewed online safety as essential as locking doors at night. Imagine if companies and governments treated cybersecurity not as a cost but as a shared responsibility.

We have the opportunity to build that future. But it begins with each of us. It begins with families like the one in Texas who decided to turn fear into action. It begins with you choosing to make habits like app hygiene, strong passwords, and suspicious-activity awareness part of your daily routine.

The threats are real, and they will continue to evolve. But so will our defenses. We have tools, knowledge, and habits that work. And more importantly, we have the ability to spread that knowledge—to create a culture where cybersecurity is not a mystery but a normal part of life.

CHOOSING ACTION

As you close this book, I want you to remember one thing: You are not powerless.

Yes, attackers are clever. Yes, technology is changing fast. Yes, AI is rewriting the rules. But none of that erases your ability to take control. Every time you refuse to click a shady link, update your devices, or talk to your kids about online safety, you are part of the solution. Every time you share your knowledge with a friend or coworker, you're building a safer digital community.

We don't secure cyberspace by waiting for someone else to do it. We secure it by acting together—billions of small, daily choices multiplied across households, workplaces, and nations.

The road ahead will be challenging, but it will also be filled with opportunity. A safer, more resilient digital world isn't just possible—it's within our reach. The question is whether we'll choose to build it.

So let's choose wisely. Let's choose awareness. Let's choose action. Let's choose to make cyberspace a place where we can all live, work, and raise our families without fear.

The future is unwritten. The pen is in our hands.

ABOUT THE AUTHOR

Dr. Eric Cole is a cybersecurity expert, entrepreneur, public figure, and bestselling author. Dr. Cole has built a solid reputation in the cybersecurity industry over the last three decades. His career has advanced from starting as a professional hacker for the CIA to becoming the forty-fourth president's commissioner on cybersecurity. His accomplishments have earned him an induction into the Information Security Hall of Fame, and he has been recognized as a Cyber Wingman by the US Air Force. His recognition has caught the interest of current clients, who include international banking institutions, Fortune 500 organizations, Bill Gates, and Saudi Aramco. His entrepreneurial accomplishments include three successful exits building eight-, nine-, and ten-figure organizations. Secure Anchor Consulting is his fourth cybersecurity business venture. Aside from his seasoned technical expertise, Dr. Cole is a well-known public figure and author of various publications. He recently released his eighth book, *Cyber Crisis*, which debuted at #1 on the *Wall Street Journal's* bestseller list. Dr. Cole's accomplishments are consequential to fulfilling his goal of providing leadership in cybersecurity, and his mission: to make cyberspace a safe place to live, work, and raise a family.